AF600502

CANONICAL ELECTIONS

Dissertation

SUBMITTED TO THE FACULTY OF THEOLOGY OF
THE CATHOLIC UNIVERSITY OF AMERICA

IN PARTIAL FULFILLMENT OF THE REQUIREMENTS
FOR THE DEGREE

DOCTOR OF CANON LAW

By DANIEL M. GALLIHER, O. P., J. C. L.
Catholic University of America

1917

Nihil Obstat:

✠ THOMAS J. SHAHAN, S. T. D.,
Censor Deputatus.

Imprimatur:

✠ J. CARD. GIBBONS,
Archiepiscopus Baltimorensis.

Approbatio Ordinis

Nihil Obstat:

FR. JOSEPHUS KENNEDY, O. P., S. T. M.
FR. AUGUSTINUS WALDRON, O. P., S. T. M.

Imprimatur:

FR. RAYMUNDUS MEAGHER, O. P., S. T. L.,
Prior Provincialis.

The Rosary Press, Somerset, Ohio
1917

CANONICAL ELECTIONS

CONTENTS

Introduction 5

Historical Concept 7

Juridical Concept 21

Qualifications of Electors 31

Convocation of Electors 45

Persons Eligible 54

The Act of Election 67

Postulation 83

Defects in Election 87

Subsequent Acts 96

Appendix—I. Manner of Electing a Sovereign Pontiff 104

II. Method of Selecting Bishops in the United States 107

Sources and Bibliography 111

INTRODUCTION

There is no institution, perhaps, that occupies a more prominent place in the entire history of ecclesiastical legislation than canonical election. For the Church during the almost twenty centuries of her active life has promulgated for no other institution such a vast and varied array of enactments, decrees, and constitutions. This ancient method of ecclesiastical provision—established by the Twelve in the designation of their successors—at times almost lost itself in the perilous conditions and numerous persecutions of the early Church, only to come forth time after time with renewed strength and vigor. During the first centuries of the Christian era the system remained weak, unstable, and undetermined. And even long after peace had been established in the Church, it failed to take on a definite form. The Church by her laws and decrees had continually endeavored to place canonical election on a firm and orderly basis, but through circumstances of times, places, and persons, her efforts were frustrated, and it was not until the celebration of the Fourth Lateran Council in 1215 that she succeeded in accomplishing her end.

Canonical elections in the early Church were limited to the designation of the successors of Saint Peter, and to the nomination of bishops. But the rise and growth of religious orders occasioned an extension in the discipline of canonical election, which became the natural and ordinary way of selecting religious superiors. The method adopted by religious institutes was later introduced into the chapters of the secular clergy. The chapters of cathedral churches not only obtained the exclusive right of electing bishops, but also of providing for other dignities and capitular offices by canonical election.

And after weathering the storms of twenty centuries the institution of canonical election still occupies an important position in the ecclesiastical discipline of today. For not only Roman Pontiffs, but also many bishops are thus chosen. Vicar capitulars are placed over vacant sees by canonical election of cathedral chapters. This mode of provision is also used to a large extent among regulars and in congregations of men and women under simple vows. But perhaps nowhere does it obtain with more accuracy and universality than in the distinctively democratic legislation of the Order of Friars Preachers, where not only generals and provincials, but even local prelates are canonically elected.

The writer, having the happy privilege of belonging to this religious institute, in which canonical election with all its solemnity plays so prominent and important a role, has thought it well worth the while to make a careful study of the legislation on the matter. It is well nigh impossible to find a clear and concise notion of the doctrine, for the various decrees and constitutions dating far back into the centuries are filled with innumerable difficulties and obscurities. The subject is too vast and extensive to allow a complete exposition of it within the limits of this dissertation, but the more important features pertaining to the matter have been carefully set forth. Avoiding wearisome and confusing details, the writer has tried to set forth whatever is included in the sacred canons as briefly and as clearly as the matter itself may allow.

The subject will be treated under the following heads: I. The historical and juridical concepts of canonical election. II. The conditions for active and passive voice. III. The forms of election and vitiating circumstances. IV. Subsequent acts. V. The present discipline of electing a Roman Pontiff, and the recent legislation on the method of proposing candidates for bishoprics in the United States.

CHAPTER I

Historical Concept

Just as Christ, Our Lord, freely called the apostles to the work of the apostolate and constituted them the first pastors of the Church, so also the apostles themselves placed others over the churches they had founded. The first election conducted by the apostles was that of Matthias. Peter rising up in the midst of his brethren reminded them that they must choose a successor for the apostolate of Judas and that this successor must be chosen from those who had accompanied Jesus in His journeys among men and who had witnessed His ascent into heaven. The Scriptures go on to tell us that two were appointed: Joseph and Matthias and that the lot fell upon Matthias and he was numbered with the eleven apostles.[1] Peter alone of all the apostles had ordinary power over the entire Church and consequently his power alone was handed down to his successors—the extraordinary jurisdiction enjoyed by the other apostles expired with them. Thus the Roman Pontiff alone, the successor of Peter, could constitute bishops with the same right by which Peter had constituted them. This was the most ancient discipline of the Church.

In the course of time when episcopates had been instituted, their regions were extended and provinces were divided. This rendered the appointing of bishops slow and difficult and since the good of the Church demanded a modification of discipline, the Holy See committed the right of election to the people, clergy and bishops of the different churches. So in the early ages of the Church elections contained these three elements: the people, the clergy and the bishops. The people presented the candidates and furnished testimony as to their fitness; the clergy voted on them, and the bishops confirmed and consecrated them. Of greater moment, however, was the suffrage of the clergy than the testimony of the people. But of still greater account was the authority of the bishops assembled in provincial synods, hearing, weighing, now approving, now rejecting the votes of the clergy and the testimony of the people. Saint Cyprian[2] says that the supreme power of electing candidates worthy of the

---

[1] Acts I.

[2] L. I. Ep. 4.

episcopate and of rejecting the unworthy, lies with the people, but in these words is signified only the conscience and testimony of the people, who are better acquainted with the virtues and vices of the candidates. Many things concerning the candidates, of which the people were well aware, were unknown to the bishops. With the freedom, therefore, and the necessity of making known whatever they knew of the morals and the actions of those who were invited to the episcopate, elections appeared to be in the power of the people. The testimony of the people, however, was not unquestionable, but frequently uncertain, inconstant, divided and corrupted, hence the supreme power of examining, approving and disapproving always lay with the bishops, by whose judgment episcopal elections finally became orderly and constant.

It is certain that orders inferior to the episcopate pertained to the will and power of the bishops, although they were not conferred upon any one without consulting the clergy and the people. Bishops, therefore, enjoyed the right and power to choose clerics and beneficiaries of their own churches, but since circumstances prevented them from knowing the morals and ability of the candidates, they were forced to rely upon the testimony of the clergy and the people. When, however, the piety and morals of the candidate were so manifest, that no further testimony was needed, the bishop would ordain him and then notify the clergy and the people of the fact. Thus Cornelius tells us that Theoctistus, Bishop of Caeserea, ordained Origen in 218 A. D.[1] And in like manner Cyprian ordained Aurelius, who later (388) became the illustrious archbishop of Carthage.[2]

After the time of Constantine, the people still continued to have a part in episcopal elections.[3] In the Second Council of Carthage, 217 A. D., provincial bishops were forbidden to ordain one whom the people presented, unless he were confirmed by the metropolitan.[4] The Third Council of Carthage, 251 A. D., decreed that if two or three bishops elected a candidate, he might be ordained provided he could exonerate himself before the people of all the crimes with which he was charged.[5] Of such regard were the good morals of the elect, that they must have as many witnesses as there were voices among the people. The Fourth Council of Carthage, 252 A. D., drew up a formula to examine the faith

[1] Eusebius VI. n. 23.
[2] Epistles of Cyprian, Book 3, n. 22.
[3] Optatus, L. I.
[4] C. 12.
[5] C. 40.

and morals of the bishops elect, but the clergy and people assenting, this could be omitted and the elect consecrated with the consent and in the presence of the metropolitan. Provision was made in the Fifth Council of Carthage, 253 A. D., lest the bishop to whom the government of a vacant see had been entrusted should be elected to that see, no matter how much the people might desire it.

Thus through the first five centuries the principal part in episcopal elections was taken by the bishops, more especially by the metropolitan. The history of these centuries tells of many instances of episcopal elections, which neither the clergy nor the people desired.[1] Leo I in very forceful words forbade the bishops to accede to the tumultuous postulations of the people or to be influenced by the votes of an unlettered and violent multitude. The same Pontiff prescribed that where the votes of the electors were divided, the metropolitan should give the bishopric to the one who excelled in merit and virtue. This right alone belonged to the people that there could be forced upon them no bishop whom they had continually refused and whom they were unwilling to receive, and secondly, that the obedience which they were to render should be in accordance with christian liberty. To these two considerations the bishops could limit them in elections.

During these centuries not only bishops, clerics and the laity, but princes and emperors were important factors in episcopal elections. It seemed to the Roman Pontiffs and the bishops that christian nobles and magistrates should be worthy of more consideration than the people, and that their part in the suffrage should be of greater import. This must not be imputed to unseemly adulation or partiality to worldly potentates, but it simply signified that these men were eminent not only for power and birth but for wisdom, zeal and charity to the Church far more sincere than that of the people, who were easily influenced by empty words, and led astray by the hope of gain. And if the Church thought fit to make concessions to the nobles and magistrates, for a greater reason was it proper that she should make more ample concessions to the supreme rulers, as heads of the people and the whole republic, whose prudence and sagacity, whose love for the Church and whose power to promote the public good were greater than those of the people. If then the people were not to be excluded from the elections, neither were their princes and emperors. Although the influence of the princes in episcopal elections was incalculable and in time gave rise to many

[1] Sidonius, L. 4. Ep. 25; Ambrosius, Ep. 59, 82.

and shameful abuses, still it must here be noted that their consent never in any way affected the validity of the elections.

II. From the fifth to the eighth centuries the people and clergy enjoyed the same liberty of former ages in episcopal elections. Gregory the Great, writing to the Duke of Campania, says that the primates of Naples should invite the people to take part in the elections of other bishops, and if there was no one in Naples worthy of episcopal dignity, they should send to Rome the names of three men of learning and approved morals, from whom a bishop would be chosen with the consent of the whole city.[1] Although the dukes, governors of the city, the nobility of the provinces and later on the senate and the people played an important part in elections, still by far the principal actors were the clergy. Gregory afterwards addresses the presbyters, deacons and clergy of Milan concerning a bishop to be elected by them.[2] And writing to the bishops of Epirus, he confirmed an election made by the clergy and bishops of the province. Gregory never wished to interfere in elections except when necessity demanded. His one aim was to safeguard the rights and liberties of the churches and that every church should have for a pastor a member of its own clergy. He himself had been elected by the clergy, senate and Roman people.[3]

Pope Symmachus said that the clergy and the people should be consulted by the visiting bishop who had charge of the vacant church and the election.[4] The first synod of Rome under the same Symmachus decreed that if all the votes of the Roman clergy were unanimous for one candidate, he should be declared bishop, but if they were divided the majority should prevail. The words of this synod seem to imply that the clergy alone enjoyed suffrage, but it is generally admitted that the people also shared this suffrage. Pope Hormisda states that in elections the Divine Will is manifested by the voice and consent of the people.[5] Vigilius, however, was elected pope by the clergy alone.[6] In subsequent elections, the people were re-admitted; first, the clergy would elect, then the most prominent of the laity and populace would give their consent. Sergius was raised to the pontifical throne by the clergy, people and army.

[1] L. 2, Ep. 15.

[2] L. 2, Ep. 29.

[3] Joan. Diac., Vita Greg. M.

[4] Ep. 5.

[5] Ep. 25.

[6] Liberato. Breviar. C. 22.

The Second Council of Orleans decreed that the new bishops of the French church should be elected by the provincial bishops.[1] In the seventh canon of the same Council it was ordained that the bishops, clergy, and people should elect the metropolitans and the election should be celebrated in the presence of all the bishops of the province; but for the election of a bishop there should assemble only those bishops whom the metropolitan would call. The difference between the election of bishops and metropolitans was clearly defined in the Third Council of Orleans, in which it was prescribed that the votes of both the clergy and the people were essential to all elections either episcopal or metropolitan; but for the election of a bishop, the presence of one metropolitan sufficed, while for a metropolitan all the provincial bishops must be present.[2]

An additional clause to the above discipline was added in the Fifth Council of Orleans to the effect that no bishop might take possession of his see without the consent or permission of the king. In the Third Council of Paris, all elections were declared null and void, which were brought about by the authority of the prince alone, because sometimes these unreasonable monarchs not rarely abused their power to conduct elections with no intervention of the clergy or consent of the people.[3] With no less constance did the Fifth Council of Paris condemn this unlawful and violent procedure and it ordained that the successors of deceased bishops should be chosen by the metropolitan, clergy and people of the city, without any influence or bribes of secular authority; and if any election should be otherwise effected, the same should be considered invalid according to the statutes of the Fathers.[4] This statute was confirmed by a royal document of Clotaire II. There was left to the prince the privilege of confirming one whom the bishops, clergy and people had elected and also of sending a bishop from his palace to vacant churches, with the understanding that the metropolitan and bishops had the power of examining and of not ordaining him unless his virtues and merits were clearly manifest. But it cannot be denied that many princes exerted an evil influence over elections and that at times the bishops and clergy were but the medium of electing him whom the prince had already named. There were times also when the bishops invited the king to suggest the names of those whom

[1] Can. I.

[2] Can. III.

[3] Can. VIII.

[4] Can. I.

they considered fit for the episcopate—never, however, to the exclusion of the clergy's suffrage and the people's consent.

In Spain the Council of Barcelona reserved elections to the clergy and people in this way, that they might name two or three persons, from whom the metropolitan and provincial bishops would choose the one who seemed to them best fitted for the office.[1] In the same canon the intervention of royal power in the elections was clearly insinuated, but the Fifth Council of Toledo makes no reference to it and places everything in the will of the people, clergy and bishops. Martin, bishop of Braga, forbade the people to mingle in the elections, contending that bishops should be elected by bishops, as they alone were qualified to judge the fitness of candidates. But this prohibition was not enforced and the people always had a part in the elections. The bishops would listen to the wishes of the clergy and to the testimony of the people and then proceed to elect the bishop themselves. From the Fourth to the Twelfth Councils of Toledo in the year 681 there are no traces of royal interference in elections; during this interval the bishops enjoyed absolute power and even presided at the elections of the nobility.[2] Some documents of the Twelfth Council are extant, whereby the power of nominating bishops is attributed to the kings.

Augustine was constituted bishop of England by Pope Gregory and by papal command consecrated by French bishops. This method was necessarily resorted to because in the English Church —at that time springing into new life—there were no persons capable of electing a bishop. But once the Church of England was again firmly established, there are many instances of elections carried on in the ordinary manner of the times. We read in Bede's English History[3] that Saint Cuthbert was elected bishop of Lindisfarne in a council presided over by the archbishop Theodore and in the presence of King Egfrid. And so on throughout the following ages of this period, one council after another ordained that bishops should be present at all elections and if absent should be represented by letters in which their consent was expressed. But these wise regulations were not always observed and the ecclesiastical affairs of England were often in a troubled state. King Alfred sent Wilfrid, whom he had made a presbyter, to France to be consecrated by French bishops. At the same time Cead was created bishop of York by command of

[1] Can. III.

[2] Conc. Tol. VIII, Can. X.

[3] Book III, C. 22-28.

King Osuf.[1] These centuries also abound with numerous examples of royal intervention in elections.

Elections in Africa were conducted with much difficulty. The primate or metropolitan would send a provincial bishop to preside at elections. Very frequently the clergy and people had long and bitter dissensions over the proposed candidates. This, however, was the least of the troubles. Genseric, king of the Vandals, in his tyrannical and cruel persecution, drove all the bishops into exile and would not permit others to be ordained. At the request of Emperor Valentinian he consented that Deogratias be made bishop of Carthage. This bishop lived but three years and after his death no bishops were created in the proconsular province of Africa and the one time number of one hundred and sixty-four was reduced to three.[2] Genseric was succeeded by his son, Huneric, who allowed Emperor Zeno and Empress Placidia to appoint a bishop to the see of Carthage—which had been vacant for twenty-four years—on condition that the Emperor in turn would grant the Arians full liberty of religion throughout the vast empire. The bishops protested against the see of Carthage being filled at so great a sacrifice to the universal Church, but the people were enraged at this protest and proceeded to an election with such violence that the bishops were powerless either to prevent or postpone it. This state of affairs gradually became brighter, and the African bishops, choosing to obey a heavenly rather than an earthly king, elected bishops for every vacant see in the African church. They were moved by the hope that they could appease the wrath of the Vandal king, or that if the churches could not have bishops they would at least have martyrs. Hilderic, the successor of Huneric, banished all these prelates, but his successor Trasamund, desiring to reign in peace and tranquillity, permitted elections to be celebrated with absolute freedom.[3]

III. From the eighth to the tenth century elections were conducted in much the same way is in former years. Under the reign of Charlemagne unrestricted liberty prevailed. Hadrian I advised him never to interfere in the elections, and he himself set the example by declaring that he would in no way infringe upon the freedom of suffrage of the clergy and people.[4]

In Italy the bishops of Ravenna were always elected by the clergy and people, neither the legates of the Roman Pontiff nor

[1] Bede V, 20.
[2] Victor—History of Vandal Persecutions III.
[3] Ib. C. 28.
[4] Thomassin V, p. 108.

those of the king having any voice in the matter. But the archbishop of Ravenna could not ordain provincial bishops without the consent of the pope. Bishops of the province of Milan were elected by the clergy and people, confirmed by the pope and king, and ordained by the metropolitan. But by far the most prominent feature of the episcopal elections in the Italian peninsula was the authority of the bishops; we can find very few instances of any bishops having been elected without the consent of all the provincial bishops.[1]

From what has been said it can easily be seen that there is no foundation for the assertion made by Sigebert in his chronicles that Hadrian bestowed on Charlemagne the power of electing the Roman Pontiff and of investing archbishops and bishops. Sigebert published this fable for the first time three hundred and thirty years after the death of Hadrian. In the time of Charlemagne the question of investitures was not dreamed of, but in the time of Sigebert the whole world was aroused over it, for Emperor Henry claimed the right for himself. Furthermore, the controversy over investitures arose at a date later than that of the fictitious Roman Synod, which according to Sigebert was held in the year 774.

It is true indeed that Zachary conferred on King Pepin the power of nominating bishops, but this was nothing more than a dispensation which the nature of the troublous times demanded. We admit that San Gallensis[2] relates some episcopal appointments made by Charlemagne, but he says nothing of his reasons for thus acting; he passes over in silence the workings of ambitious men, the artifices of unscrupulous princes, the endeavors of powerful queens to have clerics of their families decorated with episcopal dignity; he does not even mention the unyielding and noble stand of Charlemagne that only pastors worthy of the high office be placed over churches. But aside from the fact that the truthfulness and authority of San Gallensis are questioned among learned men, it must furthermore be noted that the evils of the times and the varying conditions could have compelled Charlemagne not to allow the churches to remain vacant, nor to permit dissensions to be protracted. Even granting that the nominations really took place, they are facts, not rights; they are examples, not decrees.

Charlemagne conceded to the French clergy absolute freedom in episcopal elections, not as a new favor or kindness but as

[1] Du Chesne III. pp. 894-901.

[2] T. II, p. 108.

an ancient right which the sacred canons conferred, and as a liberty belonging to the Church, whose guardians and defenders kings should be. Louis the Mild began his reign by confirming the concession of Charlemagne and by granting the same liberty in the elections of abbots. Einhard in the annals of 825 A. D. relates that Drugo, brother of Louis, was canonically elected bishop of Metz by free suffrage, to which Louis gave his consent.[1] The biographer of Louis tells us that not only the emperor and clergy, but also the nobles and people took part in the election of Drugo. The metropolitan invested the bishop by placing in his hands a staff, then the ceremony was immediately repeated by the emperor at the request of the metropolitan. Thus from these friendly relations between ecclesiastical and secular power began investiture by the emperor, which in later years caused long and bitter conflicts between popes and emperors.

Although in the elections of these times the clergy frequently prevailed over the people and sometimes the people over the clergy, canonical freedom always remained intact. When the kings interfered liberty still obtained, for they either approved of the one chosen by the clergy and people, or proved to them the fitness of those of their own choice. Of such a nature was the election of Drugo.

The peace and concord that prevailed in the reigns of Pepin, Charlemagne, Louis the Mild and Charles the Bald did not continue under their successors. The latter pretended that they were heirs not only to the kingdom, but also of royal veneration and deference throughout the extent of the universal Church. But conditions were greatly bettered by the prudence and firmness of Hincmar, archbishop of Rheims. He wrote to the youthful kings Louis and Caroloman, reminding them how favorably disposed he had been to their promotion and coronation, but he did not hesitate to say what were the limits of royal and ecclesiastical authority, and how willingly secular power should bow to the authority of the Church of the ages, and that they were bound in conscience not to protract the widowhood of churches, either by preventing elections or unreasonably objecting to those already held.[2] After the reigns of Charles the Fat and Charles the Simple peace and liberty were to a great extent restored in canonical elections.

Towards the end of this period wars were breaking out and raging on all sides, but the voice and authority of the canons were

[1] Du Chesne, Ib. p. 302.

[2] Flodoard III, c. 19.

held in honor; and when the majesty of the French kings was everywhere assailed by insolent tyrants, it was cherished most religiously by the Church, which permitted no bishops to be placed over them against their will. And although bishops could not take possession of their sees without the kings' consent and assistance, this was not injurious to the free elections previously concluded, for if the royal ministers would dare to hold an election themselves, it was pronounced a violation of the canons and immediately condemned.[1]

The elections in Spain were principally conducted by the provincial bishops or by those of another province. There was some interference from the people and royalty but it did not prevail over the authority of the bishops. Some say that the illustrious Eulogius was elected archbishop of Toledo by the voice of the people, but his biographer attributes his election to the bishops alone.[2]

In England, too, the authority of the bishops in ecclesiastical elections far outweighed that of the people, clergy and royalty. When the clergy, monks and canons were each striving to place a bishop on the episcopal throne of Winchester, Dunstan, archbishop of Canterbury, put an end to the controversy by appointing Elphege, just as he had appointed his predecessor Ethelwold. In the biography of Saint Dunstan, the author ascribes the power of electing bishops to the kings. Such, however, was not the general rule. King Edgar did nominate Dunstan to the see of Worcester in 957, and the bishopric of London becoming vacant a short time after, he was compelled at the same time also to govern that diocese. Dunstan afterwards appointed Oswald as his successor in the see of Worcester. Finally Dunstan was raised to the metropolitan see of Canterbury by the unanimous consent of the adjacent churches and people.[3] These few excerpts from the life of Saint Dunstan show the common practice of providing for vacant churches during this period.

IV. At the close of the tenth century episcopal elections in the Western Church embraced these three elements: the principal electors were bishops, the clergy exercised more power than the people, the consent of the king was necessary. The people from now on gradually lost their hold and the last instance we find of their enjoying active voice was in the twelfth century.[4]

[1] Du Chesne, Ib., p. 489.
[2] Hispan. Illust. III, p. 894.
[3] Thomassin, Ib., p. 151.
[4] Ib. c. 32, n. 14.

In the year 1215 the Fourth Lateran Council under Innocent III excluded the people and provincial bishops from episcopal elections, and reserved them to cathedral chapters. It is much controverted as to when the intervention of the royalty was removed. Some hold that it was at the time of the Second Lateran Council in 1139, when elections were reserved to the bishops and clergy; others—and more probably—that from the twelfth to the fourteenth centuries royalty through custom gave way to laws which reserved elections to the diocesan clergy, and consequently to the chapters of cathedral churches. Clement V in the year 1305 reserved to himself appointments to vacant bishoprics in the diocese of Rome.

The successors of Clement V and Benedict XII reserved the elections of all bishops throughout the Church to the Holy See. The reason for this reservation lies in the fact that many evils had crept into the elections, which evils had arisen from the ambition of men, from dissensions among those who enjoyed the privilege of suffrage and from the unlawful means employed to obtain possession of episcopal sees. And since it fell to the Supreme Pontiff to supply a remedy for these evils, thus it was that he reserved the right of election to himself, hoping thereby to heal the dissensions and to promote the common good of the Church.[1]

The Holy See in no way usurped rights that did not belong to it—as some have wrongfully contended, but merely exercised its own right, which the welfare of the Church and the nature of the times demanded that it exercise. For in the first ages of the Church, as we have shown above, the right of constituting bishops belonged to the Roman Pontiff alone, who for just reasons had conceded this power to the people, clergy, bishops and metropolitans. Since all these abused the power so graciously conceded, since they paid no attention whatever to the prescribed laws, since they were dominated by ambition, simony and unlawful desires, it was but right and just that the power of creating bishops should return to him in whom this power had ever resided, and from whom his inferiors had derived it.[2] Thus by the law of devolution for just and serious reasons the ancient discipline by which the Supreme Pontiff constituted bishops again prevailed.

It was not long before fresh troubles arose from this mode of procedure. These troubles were happily ended by means of concordats, that is, agreements entered into between the Apos-

[1] Leo X. Const. "Primitiva."

[2] Ben. XIV, Const. "In postremo."

tolic See and the most powerful princes of Europe. Nicholas V made such a concordat with the German Empire, in virtue of which German bishops were elected by the canons, but confirmed by the Holy See.[1] Leo X, after the abrogation of the pragmatic sanction, which the pseudo-council of Basle had edited against the pontifical reservations, permitted the king of France to name a worthy candidate, whom the pope in the following consistory would create bishop of the church for which he had been named.[2] Finally other pacts were entered into, or indults or privileges were conceded to the kings of Spain, Portugal, Panonia and to other princes, whereby they might nominate or present worthy candidates for their own cathedral churches.[3]

In the course of time, either through custom or through privilege, other modifications were introduced and today there are four ways of electing bishops. First, by free collation of the Roman Pontiff, which obtains in Italy, Mexico, in provinces governed by Vicars Apostolic and in France since the violation of the concordat in 1905. Secondly, by the recommendation of several candidates, made by provincial bishops or by the clergy of a widowed church. This method is practiced in Belgium, Canada, England, Holland, Ireland, the United States and in regions subject to the Sacred Propaganda. Thirdly, by the presentation of a candidate by a prince or patron. This privilege is enjoyed in Austria, Bavaria, Spain, Peru, Portugal and Servia. Fourthly, by canonical election which prevails in the Austrian archdioceses of Olmütz and Salzburg, in the dioceses of Saint Gallo, Coire and Basle in Switzerland, in some States of Germany—notably in the ecclesiastical province of the Upper Rhine, and in Prussia.

V. Papal elections have varied considerably at different periods in the history of the Church. Until the fourth century they were conducted in the same manner as episcopal elections.[4] After this time the kings and princes of Italy began to take a prominent part not only in the elections of bishops, but even in those of the Roman Pontiff. Odoacer, King of Herculi, who usurped the throne of Italy in 476, declared that Simplicius previous to his death in 483 had given him permission to take part in the election of his successor, but this concession was pronounced invalid by the clergy. Symmachus, who was raised to

[1] Bull "Ad sacrament."

[2] Bull "Pastor aeternus."

[3] Ad Regul. 2. Cancellar I.

[4] S. Clement Ep. I. c. 44.

the pontifical throne in 498, decreed that no lay persons—including the royalty, should interfere with the elections. But Theodoric, king of Italy, compelled the Roman clergy to elect Felix IV; they did so on condition that henceforth they were to enjoy absolute liberty in elections. This condition was not observed, and it gradually came to pass that no one was elected who was not acceptable to the royal household. King Athalaric prescribed that on two candidates being elected by dissenting parties, the controversy should be settled in the king's palace and that the pontiff-elect should bear all the expenses—which he fixed at the sum of three thousand crowns of gold. This ordinance was confirmed by Justinian in 553. Constantine IV granted entire freedom in papal elections by removing the abuse of awaiting the confirmation of emperors, though the latter still continued to interfere during the following centuries. Nicholas II in 1059 ordained that papal elections should be held by the cardinal bishops, who should seek the assent of the Roman clergy to their choice, and have due regard for the rights of the emperor. In 1178 Alexander III reserved the right of electing a pontiff to the entire college of cardinals, thereby excluding clergy, people and and emperor. This discipline is still in force and will receive particular attention and treatment in an appendix to this paper.

We have space for but a brief notice of the much mooted historical question concerning the pope's power to nominate his own successor. Many hold he is prohibited from doing so by divine law. The principal reasons for their assertion are: first, that ecclesiastical benefices are not hereditary; secondly, that if the pope were to appoint a successor he would be exercising power after death, something forbidden by law; thirdly, contrary decrees of Boniface II, Pius IV and Paul III.

The affirmative opinion, however, seems more probable. In the first place nothing on this point has ever been determined by divine law, for neither in Sacred Scripture nor in tradition can we find the least reference to it. And if Christ had prescribed a mode of electing the Supreme Pontiff, it would not have been changed during the various periods of the Church, but would have remained always the same. To the authority of the Church, therefore, does it belong to establish a method and to change it according to the exigencies of the times. This authority is vested in the Roman Pontiff, to whom the government of the universal Church has been committed. No canonists nor theologians question this right of the Holy Father.[1]

[1] Wernz II., p. 651.

Furthermore, in case of real and extraordinary necessity or utility to the Church, the pope can, according to the more probable opinion, licitly and validly designate—not merely recommend—his successor.[1] For the supreme and absolute power of the pope is not restricted either ex natura rei or by any special divine law to mere legislation on the nomination of a successor. It seems, therefore, that the denial of the pope's right to extend his power to the immediate nomination of a successor lacks solid foundation.

The negative arguments at the most prove that a pope cannot licitly use this mode of provision as something ordinary, nor validly impose it on a successor as an ordinance of law.[2] Sacred Scripture and divine tradition furnish no arguments to show that any restriction has been placed on pontifical authority by divine law. Nowhere did Christ by an explicit, special law forbid His vicar on earth to appoint a successor. We admit that benefices are not hereditary, but this argument has no force here, for elections exclude heredity. We grant that a Pope cannot exercise his power after death, but to elect a successor is to complete the act during life, and to suspend its effect—which is permissible. Another argument in our favor is the fact that in 1883 a Benedictine abbot found in the library of the chapter of Novara a document—which every one admits as authentic—from which it is clear that Felix IV (526-530) designated as his successor Boniface II and that he did not recall this designation before his death. Boniface II himself acted in a like manner, even though he afterwards revoked his appointment. The contention that the negative is the more probable opinion is based on a false supposition, for no common opinion exists, and there are many learned doctors such as Bonacina, Decius, Ledesma, Mendoza, Suarez, Vasquez, Victoria, Wernz and others who teach the affirmative. The alleged decrees of Boniface II, Pius IV—which was never promulgated—and Paul III are opposed by that of Felix IV; besides they are not dogmatic definitions but disciplinary statutes.[3]

[1] Hefele II, p. 627; Hollweck, t. 74, p. 329.

[2] Ib.

[3] Wernz, Ib.

CHAPTER II

Juridical Concept

The word election is of Latin origin (electio, from eligere, to choose from), and in a broad sense means a choice among many persons, things, or sides to be taken. In the strict juridical sense it signifies the choice of one person among many for a definite charge or function.[1] In ecclesiastical law the sacred canons, speaking of election in its broadest sense, include also collation or mere gratuitous institution. Election thus understood is the promotion of a person to an ecclesiastical dignity or benefice, and it is properly called election, because a superior in conferring a dignity or benefice upon a person chooses him in preference to others. In a broad sense ecclesiastical election comprehends not only election strictly so-called, but also nomination, postulation, and presentation.

The essence of election in its broad sense is made manifest by showing how it differs from collation. In the first place election essentially differs from collation in this that collation is the act of a superior conferrng an ecclesiastical office, while election is an act of subjects naming a person for an office. Secondly, collation confers upon the nominee the office itself (jus in re), and in virtue of his acceptance he immediately becomes absolute master, even before he has taken actual possession; election gives but a claim to the office (jus ad rem), conferring actual possession only on the confirmation or institution of a superior.[2] Although by election the elect sometimes acquires the benefice or prelacy immediately, as do newly elected popes and generals of Orders, this does not pertain to those elections because they are elections, but because they are such elections as are confirmed by common law as soon as they are lawfully concluded and the elect consents thereto. For as soon as an elect consents to a lawful election in which he was elected, v. g., to the pontificate, he thereby from divine institution becomes the vicar of Christ and successor of Peter. A third difference is that the appointee, having once consented, is no longer free to renounce the office without the consent of his superior; on the other hand an elect may freely renounce it at any time before confirmation or institu-

[1] Boudinhon, Cath. Encycl. v. Election.

[2] Rodriq. lib. 2, q .51, a. 1.

tion.[1] Thus election taken in this way may be defined as a provision whereby subjects, in virtue of a right given them by the Apostolic See, canonically elect a certain person or persons to a vacant ecclesiastical dignity or benefice, which either the one named or one of those named shall receive by the confirmation or institution of a superior. In this definition the genus is provision, for provision is a general name given to all methods of providing for vacant offices. The essential difference between election and collation is also clearly shown, for collation is the act of a superior, election of inferiors or subjects.

Thirdly, election is taken in a more specific and proper sense, as distinguished from presentation. Election differs from presentation first not in respect to the person elected but to the electors. It implies a power of ecclesiastical office, which a layman cannot exercise. Although this power is neither of orders nor of jurisdiction, but of office,[2] it is, however, the act of an ecclesiastic, which act is reduced to the power of jurisdiction, of which a layman is wholly incompetent. Presentation on the contrary is merely the exercise of the right of patronage (jus patronatus), which may be conceded to the laity. Hence electors to ecclesiastical offices must be clerics, whereas patrons may be either seculars or ecclesiastics. The right of the candidate either in election or in presentation is the same (jus ad rem).

A second difference between election and presentation is that the former calls for canonical approbation or confirmation, while the latter leads to canonical institution by a competent superior. Although institution in a broad sense is the same as collation, in a strict sense, it is different, for collation is a free donation, whereas institution is a necessary appointment of the candidate—if fit and worthy—presented by a patron. Canonists distinguish free and necessary collation; the first is collation in the proper sense of the word, the second is properly called institution. By free collation the collator not only has the right to appoint but also to designate or nominate the person he wishes to appoint. In necessary collation the appointment belongs to one person, the designation or nomination to another, and the collator must of necessity appoint the person designated or presented to him by the patron unless canonical obstacles forbid the appointment.[3]

Election and presentation differ thirdly in this that election is vested in a number of electors, presentation in one person only

[1] Donatus, in prax. par. 3, tract. 1, q. 1, n. 8.

[2] Azorius, P. II, lib. 1, c. 14, q. 14.

[3] Smith, Elements of Ec. Law, I, p. 134.

—physical or moral. Election pertains to the members of a college, and thus understood is defined: a provision by which inferior clerics, in virtue of papal concession, canonically elect a certain person or persons to a vacant ecclesiastical charge or function, the one named or one from those named obtaining the office by the confirmation of a competent superior. Election taken in this sense agrees with collation and presentation in so far as it is a canonical provision. It differs from collation because it pertains to inferiors, while collation pertains to a superior; it differs from presentation, for presentation belongs to one person only, physical or moral, and leads to canonical institution, while election is committed to a number of clerics and calls for confirmation.

Finally election in its strict and most proper sense is distinguished from postulation and nomination. Canonists commonly define election thus understood as the canonical choice by legitimate electors of a fit person for an ecclesiastical dignity or fraternal society.[1] To this definition some think should be added the words: by the confirmation of a competent superior. Election taken in this sense differs from postulation not in regard to the electors, but as regards the person elected, for postulation, as we shall explain below, is the choice of a person juridically ineligible by reason of some canonical impediment from which the superior is requested to dispense him, while election is the appointment of a fit person. It is distinguished from nomination in this that the latter is the canonical act by which two or more fit persons are proposed to the free choice of a superior, while the former is the designation of one only.

Baldus[2] defines election differently saying that it is properly regulated determination of the will of a competent number to a person, who is chosen for a prelacy or rectorship. This definition would be clearer and more accurate if it said that election is a properly regulated determination of the will of an ecclesiastical college to a fit person, who is elected to a prelacy, rectorship, or ecclesiastical benefice, to be confirmed by a competent superior. Thus there is explained the nature of election both in respect to the elector and to the person elected, and likewise the form of election both natural, which consists in the free consent of the electors, as well as canonical, which is determined by the sacred canons, and there is also shown what sort of a right is

[1] Hostiensis Summa, tit. de electione;
Panormitanus, Rubr. de postulat. n. 2.

[2] de elect. c. 1, n. 1.

obtained from election, namely a weak and unstable right needing the strength of confirmation.

Election so defined is distinguishable into many species both as regards the electors and officers or benefices which are provided for by election. Hence diverse methods and forms of electing have been established according to the condition of the different offices to be filled. But abstracting from this diversity, that election is one essentially and specifically, which is the provision of inferior clerics, whereby, in virtue of a right conceded by the Holy See, they name a definite person to an ecclesiastical benefice, and especially to a dignity or prelacy, thus giving to the person elected a claim to the benefice (jus ad rem), which will pass into his possession by the confirmation of his superior, if the election be legitimately conducted according to canonical form.

Postulation is distinguished into simple and solemn postulation. Simple postulation is a petition made to a superior to permit one of his subjects to be elected or confirmed, or to permit said subject to consent to his election or confirmation. This method of postulation is employed in the election of religious to dignities outside their Orders, and in those of prelates of one church or diocese to an office or benefice in another church or diocese. This species of postulation has no force except when the candidate has been elected or solemnly postulated, for solemn postulation agrees with election in this that if admitted the person thus postulated has a claim to the prelacy.

Solemn postulation, however, is not election taken in its proper sense, but on the contrary far different from it. Hostiensis and Sylvius define postulation as a petition presented to a competent ecclesiastical superior, that he may provide for a certain ecclesiastical office by promoting to it a person who is prevented from being elected not on account of a personal fault or vice, but on account of some canonical impediment, which is usually dispensable and which does not render him strictly ineligible. This definition differs somewhat from that of Panormitanus[1] who says that postulation is a request made to a superior to promote a certain person to a prelacy, to which by reason of some defect or impediment he could not have been elected or promoted according to common law. Some canonists hold this second definition, but Sylvius chooses the first which is better, because it expresses that postulation has no place where the defect or impediment in the candidate is a personal vice; this is not expressed in the second, which, unless it be reduced to the sense of the

[1] Rubr. de post.

first, is incomplete and false, for according to this definition even one laboring under a personal defect could be elected, which is not true. Baldus[1] defines postulation in still another way as a canonical act by which a favor is requested of a competent superior that he may provide a prelate or give the chapter permission to elect one. But this definition is very general, and could be applied also to simple postulation.

From these definitions may be gleaned many essential differences between election and postulation. Election presupposes no canonical defect or impediment in the person to be elected, whereas postulation properly pertains to one who by reason of a defect which is not personal cannot be elected. If a person is canonically eligible for election, he cannot be postulated, for electors should choose for a benefice not only the one best fitted but also by the most suitable method. But election is a better mode of provision than postulation, hence an eligible person should be elected and not postulated, except in case of two candidates when one is elected and the other postulated. For two cannot be elected at the same time, but the law permits that in the election of one another may be postulated, even though the latter otherwise eligible is at present ineligible, for the reason that one has already been elected, and two cannot be elected at the same time. If, on the contrary, a person laboring under a canonical impediment should be elected, the election is always annulled, for such candidates must be chosen by postulation.

A second difference between election and postulation is that the former is a matter of justice, the latter of favor. Election confers a right (jus ad rem) on the elect, and there moreover arises between him and the benefice for which he has been chosen a bond of spiritual wedlock. Both the electors, therefore, and the person elected have a right that the election be confirmed. Hence the elect in requesting confirmation does not ask a favor, but merely seeks justice, and to use the words of John Andreas: "when the elect is fit and worthy, he can proudly appear before the superior, not even raising his head or biretta, for election is a question of justice, and not of favor, as is postulation."

From this second difference arises another, namely that postulation can be recalled by the postulators before it has been presented to the superior; the messenger sent to the superior can likewise be recalled, provided that the revocation reach him before he has presented himself before the superior. Furthermore, even if the postulation has been presented to the superior, it can

[1] Rubr. de post. n. 1.

still be recalled with his consent. But election cannot be revoked, for by virtue of election the person elected acquires a right (jus ad rem) to the charge or function for which he has been chosen, while in postulation the one postulated acquires no right whatsoever. Some object to this last statement, saying that postulation made for the utility and concord of the Church cannot be rejected.[1] Sylvius responds that where postulation is not made for reasons of concord, no right is acquired, not even by the postulators; but where postulation is made by two-thirds of the voters, those postulating acquire a right, and in this sense canonists must be understood who say that postulation made for the concord and advantage of the Church should be admitted. The person postulated, however, never acquires any right, since he has a canonical defect or impediment which renders him ineligible until he is dispensed therefrom. We shall return to this question again when treating of postulation in particular, where the many other differences between election and postulation will be explained.

Solemn and juridical nomination is also a way of providing for vacant churches. According to Hostiensis it is the canonical act by which the electors propose two or more worthy persons to the free choice of the superior, in order that he may appoint one of them to the vacant office.

There are three species of nomination. The first, consultative or simple nomination, is a voting previous to an election in which are proposed the names of several fit and worthy persons, one of whom may be elected later by the chapter. The second is intrinsic to election by secret ballot, and obtains when each of the electors names him whom he wishes to be elected; the one thus nominated has no right whatever before the announcement of the ballot of nomination, but once the ballot has been made known he acquires a certain right and the electors are no longer free to change their opinion. The third is solemn nomination, which is that defined above. The role of electors is the same as in election properly so-called.[2] It differs from election inasmuch as it does not confer on those named a real right to the benefice, but, on the contrary, the nominators may recall the nomination at any time before it is presented to the superior. For just as election can fall only on one person, so nomination cannot confer on several a real right to the benefice; on the contrary, their right is real inasmuch as it excludes third parties,

[1] Hostiensis, de elect., cap. Cum ad Monast.

[2] Boudinhon, Ib.

though none of them possesses the jus ad rem.[1] It is distinguished from postulation in this that it occupies itself with a number of persons, whereas in postulation one only is designated. Moreover, nomination does not, like postulation, concern itself with those who have canonical impediments, but with those who are strictly eligible. Hence there is no question of those named being dispensed from an impediment through the favor of a superior, but it is a matter of justice for the superior to confirm one of those named, if he be fit and worthy.

There are, therefore, three modes of provision for vacant benefices—election, postulation, and nomination—distinct from that general mode which consists in the collation of a superior, and also from another mode which is the presentation and institution of the one presented. These three agree in this that they are acts of an ecclesiastical college, and in them is usually observed the general form of electing by ballot; they do not give actual possession or dominion, but at the most election gives a claim to the benefice in the manner explained above. They are comprehended under election, as distinguished from collation and institution, but are of different species. Thus election may be considered either generically or specifically; considered generically postulation and nomination are species of election, but considered specifically they are species distinct from it.

In addition to these ways of providing for vacant churches or benefices, Barbosa[2] adds two others: simple petition and translation. Simple petition, since it has no foundation in law, is not an ecclesiastical provision, but merely a simple supplication by which the clergy or people beg the Holy See to grant them the prelate they desire. Neither does translation bespeak a special way of providing for a widowed church, unless accidentally and in respect to the term a quo. For it is purely accidental to the church, that its prelate was previously a bishop or a prelate of some other church; the church itself is not provided for except by institution, election, or postulation. Boudinhon includes still another method under election, namely recommendation, which is the designation of one or several fit persons made to the superior by certain members of the clergy, chiefly in view of sees to be filled. Those recommending do not act as electors, hence the persons designated acquire no real right, the Holy See remaining perfectly free to make a choice outside of the list proposed. Hence there are but two general ways of providing for widowed

[1] Ib.

[2] De jure eccles. I, c. 19, n. 2.

churches: by collation and election generically taken, which is divided into election strictly so-called, postulation, and nomination. Presentation is also included under election in a general way, as we have explained above.

Having explained the different ways in which election may be taken, it now remains to treat of the species of election strictly so-called. The Decretals[1] admit three forms or modes of electing prelates: the ordinary way by ballot, and two exceptional ways, namely, compromise and quasi-inspiration, often called common inspiration. The Council of Trent[2] abrogated the forms by compromise and quasi-inspiration in the elections of regulars, but they still find place in other canonical elections, as is clear from the constitution of Pius X, "Vacante Sede Apostolica," in which this threefold form is expressly mentioned.

Some ask whether, notwithstanding the Tridentine restriction, regulars can elect by compromise united with scrutiny. We think that since this form of compromise is not distinguished from election by ballot, or at least obtains the end of secret scrutiny, which is to exclude coercion and violation of liberty, it can reasonably be said that this form was not abrogated by the Council, for in it is strictly observed the law of secret ballot, as we shall show at length on a later page.

It has been said that election by inspiration, because it comes from the Holy Ghost, is not subject to human law. Sigismund[3] distinguishes inspiration from quasi-inspiration. The former occurs when the electors, observing no order and quasi-intoxicated, spontaneously name a person and acclaim him elected, as happened in the elections of the saintly bishops, Martin and Ambrose; the latter is when all the electors suddenly, quickly, but orderly—that is, one after another elect the same persons. Having given this distinction, he says that inspiration is not a form of election. But inspiration is from the Holy Ghost, so when evident, election by inspiration will be confirmed. Hence it is not subject to the law or form prescribed in the chapter "Quia propter."

The above remarks are true only where election by inspiration or quasi-inspiration has not been abrogated by the Council of Trent, they have no reference to the elections of regulars, where elections not conducted by secret ballot are invalid. Although what proceeds from the Holy Ghost is subject to no

---

[1] cap: Quia propter, Lateran Council, 1215, A. D.

[2] Sess. 25, de Regular. c. 6.

[3] dub. 2.

human law, this is true only where it is manifest beyond question that the Holy Ghost wills something. We cannot say, however, that inspiration from the Holy Ghost directs an election from the sole fact that it is brought about by the spontaneous and unanimous acclamations of the electors. Thus the Church will not ratify such an election, knowing full well that if it is prompted by the Holy Ghost, the electors will confirm it by secret vote, the same Holy Spirit interiorly moving and inspiring them to do so.

We can also deduce that the method of nomination was likewise excluded in the elections of regulars, since nomination is a certain species of compromise. Nomination, however, by way of compromise united to scrutiny would be valid, for the electors can nominate certain ones by secret votes, and compromise with the superior to grant them the candidate of his choice.[1] But if this nomination be referred to the superior orally and not by secret ballot, it is worthless and can be recalled even after it has been presented to the superior. It would be valid by reason of devolution, if meanwhile the electors were to elect no one else within the allotted time. It would also be valid by way of cession, for to surrender one's right is not to elect; and the electors could unanimously give up their right on the condition that the superior choose one of those named.[2]

The Council not only decreed all elections of regulars other than by secret ballot null and void, but it also ordained that any person who would allow himself to be created provincial, abbot, or prior in such a way, is deprived forever of passive voice in religion. The censure is not expressly inflicted upon generals, and since it is a question of penalty, the election of a general by public voting is indeed ipso facto invalid, but the general-elect does not incur the censure. One is said to give permission to one's election to a prelacy, who consents either antecedently or subsequently thereto.

In a word the only point insisted upon by the Council of Trent was that the elections of regulars should be by secret scrutiny, in such a way, that the votes of the electors would never become known.

In the Order of Friars Preachers there can be no question of election by compromise or by common inspiration. The early Constitutions[3] approve of the triple form contained in the chapter "Quia propter." But the Roman edition says: "We declare

[1] Passerini, De electione canonica, c. I, n. 64.

[2] Ib.

[3] dist. 2, cap. 2, text. 1 .

this ancient form of election has already been abolished by the Council of Trent, and in every canonical election of our Order the decree of the Sacred Council must be observed."[1] And immediately after this text is inserted an excerpt from the Chapter of Bologna, 1564: "Regarding the execution of the Tridentine decree, we command all our brothers that in future elections the form here given must be observed. Let each of the electors write the name of a candidate on a schedule or have it written, but the elector's name shall never be written, and it shall not be revealed either to the scrutineers or to the one confirming. Election by common inspiration and compromise having therefore been abolished, election by scrutiny must always be observed." From this, then, it is clear that in the Order of Friars Preachers there can be no canonical election except by scrutiny, and in order that for the future the form of electing prelates in the Order would be firm, stable and certain, the capitulars of Bologna not only ordained that every canonical election should be by scrutiny, but they even decreed the form of such elections.

[1] d. II, c. II.

CHAPTER III

Qualifications of Electors

The end of canonical election is to provide fit and worthy prelates or superiors for ecclesiastical colleges. Hence bishops, generals, abbots, provincials, local prelates, dignitaries of cathedrals, canons and the like are canonically elected, so that worthy and competent prelates or ministers may be provided for various ecclesiastical charges or functions. From this final cause, which is the first cause, follows the efficient cause. And since election is an act, its efficient cause are agents or electors, who to elect validly, must be possessed of certain qualities, determined either by common law, or by particular statutes of the different churches or institutes. In the present chapter, we shall occupy ourselves especially with an exposition of those qualities or conditions, which electors must necessarily have in order lawfully and validly to take active part in canonical elections.

Elections belong strictly speaking to the college or community for which a prelate is to be elected.[1] This ordinance of common law has been adopted by the greater number of religious orders, in which, according to the statutes of the respective orders, either all the prelates—even local—are elected by the particular convents, as in the Order of Friars Preachers; or provincials by provincial chapters; or generals by a general congregation, as in the Society of Jesus. Either, therefore, prelates are not elected, but instituted by supreme authority, as for instance, the pope very frequently institutes bishops, or if elected, they are elected by those colleges over which thy are chosen to preside, unless custom, privilege, or the will of higher authority dispose otherwise.

Some canonists hold that at least three persons are required to constitute a college.[2] Others, on the contrary, say that two suffice.[3] The latter seems to be the more probable opinion, for in the chapter "Nullus"[4] we read: "Let no presbyter be elected in a church whose congregation numbers two or three, except

---

[1] Cap. Congregatio 43. q. 7.

[2] Sylvius, Cap. 1 de electione; Castell, de elect. c. 5, n. 43; Donatus, tract. 4, q. 6, n. 3.

[3] Innoc. Cap. dilecto; Jo. And. c. statutum; Rodriq. II, q. 53, a. III. Barbosa, c. 1. de elect. n. 3.

[4] I. de elect.

by canonical election of the same two or three." In particular law the statutes of each order must be observed.

In the Order of Friars Preachers no convent can elect a prior, unless it has three vocals (Rome, 1601). Donatus[1] adds that a general chapter cannot by its own authority establish contrary legislation. The ordination of the Chapter of Valencia (1596) which required that these vocals must have completed twelve years from profession, was replaced by one of the Chapter of Rome (1608) which reduced the requirement to six years. The ancient discipline of the Chapter of Valencia was restored by the Chapter of Louvain (1885), but again modified by the Chapter of Avila (1895), which decreed that every priest has active voice in all canonical elections, provided he shall have completed nine full years from his first profession, and have satisfied the other conditions required by law.

Camillus notes that where there are but three electors, they cannot validly elect one of their own number, because the one elected must have a majority of two votes, and this majority no one of the three can obtain unless he elect himself, which is not permitted and would render the election null.

Although at least two are required to constitute a college, still the rights of an established college can continue in one alone. If, for example, all the members of a college, one alone excepted, should die, be excommunicated, or in some other way rendered disqualified to elect, the one remaining could lawfully and validly carry on an election, provided that he would not elect himself.[2] Hence if one or two of a college of three vocals renounce their right, such renunciation can in no way prevent the one left from voting, should he wish to do so. This discipline was approved by a response of the Sacred Congregation of Bishops and Regulars, August 21, 1690, which pronounced valid and confirmed an election held in a convent of Ripano, that had been vetoed by the provincial because, one of three vocals renouncing his voice, the other two had conducted an election.

Having shown that a college of at least two or three members is necessary to hold a lawful and valid election, we shall now consider the qualifications or conditions required of vocals for the exercise of their right to vote.

1. Natural law requires that an elector be in actual possession of the full use of reason. Hence natural law excludes those who have not reached the age of puberty, the demented, those in

[1] n. 5.

[2] Sylvius, electio I. n. 2; Hostiensis, c. 2 de post.

a state of perfect intoxication, those in such a state of anger as to render full deliberation impossible. The demented or insane may validly elect during a lucid interval, but lucid intervals must not be presumed, for once insanity has taken possession of a person, it is considered to be present always, unless the contrary be proved. And if drunkenness or anger does not destroy the free use of reason, neither will either of these vices ipso facto irritate an election. Just as for contracts or promises, so also for canonical elections, that deliberation is necessary, which is required to constitute a mortal sin.[1]

The infirm, aged, blind, deaf, and the like are not unqualified for the exercise of active voice, since they can freely deliberate on the one to be elected. The blind, however, are counselled to renounce their right, and Sigismund extends this counsel to the deaf, so that they may act with a safer conscience.

II. Electors must be ecclesiastics, that is, clerics or religious, and not laymen. In elections of ecclesiastical prelates, the vote of a lay person is not only null, but it invalidates such elections. Although a layman may exercise suffrage in canonical elections by special papal privilege, they can never acquire it by custom.[2] Laymen may also be admitted, not to take active part, but to defend and protect the electors, or to see that the form is observed.

III. Only those who compose the college or community to be provided can be electors, for since election belongs per se primo to a college, it follows that they alone can elect, who are assigned to the college.

In the elections of regulars only those professed enjoy active voice, the others, not yet incorporated into religion, are not strictly speaking religious. Tacit profession is sufficient, for he who is tacitly professed, is lawfully professed, and is a member of religion provided it is evident he has completed a year of probation according to the Council of Trent.[3] Religious can elect prelates for those institutes only in which they were professed. If a religious pass to another order he cannot take part in its elections before his profession, and according to some he does not acquire active voice even after his profession.[4] It is furthermore required that the elector belong to that body in the con-

---

[1] Antoninus, Cajetan, Sylvius.

[2] D. Antoninus, I. tit. 16, c. 11; Hostiensis, de elect. n. 5; Donatus, 3, tract. 4, q. 4.

[3] Layman, IV, tract. 2, c. 12, n. 3; Lezana, v. electio, n. 2.

[4] electionibus, ex Clem.; Castell. c. 5, n. 58.

vent or monastery, in the general or provincial chapter, in the congregation or college whose office it is here and now to elect. Wherefore chaplains or perpetual beneficiaries of a cathedral, who are not members of the chapter, are not admitted to canonical elections. Lastly, to be a legitimate elector, a religious must have become so in accordance with the particular statutes of his order or institute.

Thus in the Order of Friars Preachers, to be an elector for a conventual prior, or for his companion to a provincial chapter, one must have been assigned to the convent in which the election is to take place two months before date of said election. There are, however, some exceptions to this doctrine, which will be given below.

From what has been said it follows that the religious of one convent cannot take part in the elections of another, and that a prior or local prelate of one convent cannot vote for a prior or prelate in another except by special privilege. In accordance with this statute of common law the Constitutions of the Order of Friars Preachers decree that a vocal or prior of one convent has no voice in the elections of another, unless he shall have been sent to the other as vicar of the election.[1] And since generals and provincials belong to no convent in particular, they also have no voice in the elections of conventual prelates, although according to the particular statutes of some orders they may institute said prelates. The general and provincials of the Order of Friars Preachers do not enjoy suffrage in conventual elections, but it pertains to them to confirm these elections, and in case of devolution to institute local prelates.

The vocals cannot of themselves admit an outsider to take part in an election, because a college has no power of conceding suffrage to any one, who does not already possess the faculty by papal concession.[2] This doctrine is not admitted by all, though the majority of canonists agree in this that the right of exercising active voice may be prescribed by custom. And since such a custom is contrary to common law, a prescription of forty years is required to establish it. Moreover, to prescribe a custom against common law, a colored title at least is also required. To prove this custom it is not required that the right of voting has been exercised many times during the forty years, for one act alone suffices when the one elected possesses the benefice for

[1] Passerini, De elect. can., c. 10, n. 16.

[2] Ib. n. 17.

forty years.[1] An outsider, having once prescribed the right of suffrage, may not be ejected from an election, but should be summoned. But if it chance that his vote is not numbered with the others, the election is not vitiated.

IV. The fourth condition requires electors to be present in the particular place in which the college is congregated to hold the election. For since election belongs per se to the college, no elector can take part in it unless he is collegiately present, where the college is to hold the election.

Common law forbids absent capitulars to send their votes in writing. Some canonists, however, assert that contrary.[2] Others say that a vote sent by sealed letter is not against the substance of the law, and base their opinion on this that in the Congregation of Saint John the Baptist in Portugal every religious sends by letter his vote for the election of a general. But these contrary opinions cannot be admitted, for the true doctrine is clearly expressed in the chapter "Si quis justo":[3] "An absent capitular cannot send his vote by letter, because votes must not be expressed previous to the scrutiny, but cast secretly and separately in the scrutiny itself." The mode of election practiced in the above named Portuguese Congregation adds no strength to the contrary opinion, for this was done according to a particular statute confirmed by papal authority. Custom legitimately prescribed could also permit suffrage in writing.[4] But aside from privilege or custom, absent capitulars cannot send their votes in writing, even with the consent of the chapter.[5]

The infirm, who are confined in the convent of election, have the right to vote, and the scrutineers should go to them, and receive their votes according to canonical form. Sigismund contends the same holds for those who are at a distance from the cloister, in the city for example. But others think that such electors should send a procurator.[6] We prefer the latter opinion, for it seems unreasonable that—the electors assembled and all things in readiness—the scrutineers should be held to go to the city to receive the vote of an infirm elector. But in such cases custom and the particular laws of each college must be observed.

In the Order of Friars Preachers all who are not present in the convent of election are considered to be absent.[7] Hence the

[1] Rota, decis. 548, n. 6, par. 5.
[2] Azorius, L. 13, c. 10, p. 2.; Reiff. L. 1, t. VI, n. 106.
[3] De electione in VI.
[4] cap. fin. de consuetudine.
[5] Sigis. dub. 13, n. 1; Castell. c. 5, n. 65; Barbosa, n. 17; Donatus tract. 4, q. 17.
[6] Boerius, Castell, Mandag, Sylvius.
[7] Consti. n. 546.

scrutineers are held to go only to those infirm who are confined in the convent of election. Some extend this to all electors who though present in the convent of election, are nevertheless through a just and lawful reason unable to be present in the election chamber.[1] Wherefore in this Order only those electors enjoy the right of active voice who are personally present in the convent of election.

Electors legitimately absent do not, however, want for a means of casting their votes, for common law permits them to be present by proxy. The chapter "Quia propter" lays down four conditions on this point: 1° the absentee himself must constitute the procurator; 2° he must be legitimately detained; 3° he must confirm his reason by oath, if the college so desire; 4° the procurator must be a member of the electoral college. The chapter "Si quis justo" adds three conditions more to those already given: 1° the absent elector may institute several procurators, provided that he institute them in solidum; 2° the procurator must cast the two votes for the same candidate, unless the mandate was given for a certain person—in which case he may cast his own vote for the candidate of his choice; 3° if no one from the college will accept the procuration, he cannot send an outsider without the consent of the chapter, nor can he on this account send his vote in writing.

A few things are to be noted concerning these conditions. He is considered absent, who is so distant from the place of election, that the scrutineers are not held—according to their respective statutes or customs—to go to him personally to receive his vote. Procurators can be sent by those absentees only, who are detained in a place to which a procurator can be conveniently summoned. A vocal remaining in a place to which a procurator cannot be conveniently summoned, loses the right of active voice, and need not be advised of an approaching election.[2] But he always has the right—even though the summons to election has already been given—of acceding to a place, whence he may elect or summon a procurator. Impediments constituting legitimate detention from the place of election would be grave illness, deadly enmities, imprisonment, citation to a higher tribunal, and the like. Moreover, the impediment must be such, that even at the time of election it would prevent his personal appearance. If a procurator is admitted without an oath, the chapter thereby

---

[1] Tabien., Castell.

[2] Passerini, Ib. c. 10, n. 38.

renounces its right to make exception to the reason of the vocal's absence. The college, if it please, may admit a procurator of one not detained by an impediment.[1] If the vocal should die before the election takes place, the office of procurator ceases, but if the electoral body, unaware of the vocal's death, admits the vote by proxy, the election is valid. No capitular is bound to act as procurator for an absent elector, and if an outsider is instituted, the college may refuse to admit him, if it sees fit. Although a procurator cannot cast his own vote for one candidate, and that of him whose procurator he is for another, unless the procuration has been given for a certain person, still if two candidates are equally eligible, he may in conscience cast one vote for each, unless this be forbidden by law; if, however, the two candidates are of unequal merit, the procurator is bound to cast the two votes for the more worthy. Procurators who do not belong to the college must have all the qualifications required of vocals. A procurator may sub-delegate if this faculty be conceded in the mandate, otherwise sub-delegation is doubtful and uncertain. When several procurators are instituted in solidum, "melior est conditio occupantis"; if two or more should reach the electoral chamber at the same time, that one is to be admitted, whom the chapter or majority of the chapter agrees upon, if the chapter can come to no agreement, then the one first named in the mandate is admitted.

All absent electors can elect a procurator unless prohibited by particular statute. The Sacred Congregation of the Council declared valid elections by proxy in religious institutes, unless otherwise ordained by the particular laws of the institutes.[2] In the Order of Friars Preachers absent vocals are forbidden to elect either by letter or by proxy.

V. Electors must be in sacred orders, in those of the subdiaconate at least. This condition excludes two classes of persons from elections: lay brothers and clerics not in sub-deacon's orders. Under the name of lay brothers we do not include monks or religious, who are deputed to choral duties and the divine ministry, for in ancient times these monks—even though there chanced to be priests or clerics among them—always elected their abbots. Neither do our remarks refer to those religions, military orders, for example, in which lay religious conduct the elections, but only to ecclesiastical colleges in which clerics are appointed to celebrate the divine mysteries.

[1] Ib. n. 39.
[2] Ib. n. 40.

This condition was prescribed by the following decree of the Council of Trent:[1] "For the future no one in cathedral churches or secular colleges shall have a voice in chapter—even if freely conceded by others—unless he be constituted in the order of subdiaconate at least." Some authors contend that this decree includes institutes of regulars, first because the decree speaks absolutely of all ecclesiastical colleges, and secondly because this is the general practice of religious orders.[2] But others hold the opposite, and base their opinion on a declaration of the Sacred Congregation of the Council (May 22, 1577) that religious even though not in sacred orders could have voice in elections, since the Tridentine decree did not include monasteries of regulars, but only their cathedral churches.[3] However, in this point, as well as in others, the particular laws and customs of each order must be observed.

Before passing to the next condition, we shall speak briefly on a few points that are frequently controverted among canonists. Although some hold that lay brothers and clerics not in major orders cannot by custom prescribe active voice in canonical elections,[4] still the opposite seems more probable. For the chapter "De consuetudine" says that custom reasonably and legitimately prescribed derogates from a law.[5] For what can be destroyed by a just law, can be destroyed by a just custom, which is equivalent to a just law. Secondly a cleric who during an election satisfies the required conditions—in respect to age, reception of orders, and the like—must be admitted to the election, but the electors are not held to await such a person's becoming qualified.[6] This is extended to one who by papal dispensation has been ordained before the required age. It also holds for those who have been surreptitiously and illegitimately ordained.[7] But those thus ordained are ipso facto suspended,[8] and hence must not be admitted until the suspension shall have been removed. Thirdly, a capitular having the power of jurisdiction, but not of orders, can transact those matters of election which pertain to the jurisdiction of his office, although he cannot vote in the election itself,

---

[1] sess. 22, cap. 4 de reform.

[2] Sylvius, electio I, n. 3; Suarez II, c. 4, n. 5.

[3] Tab., electio I, n. 5; Rodriq. II, q. 52, a. 5.

[4] Barbosa, c. 2, n. 3; Donatus, q. 6, n. 5.

[5] Panormitanus, Ib. n. 9; Sanchez, l. 7 de mat., d. 4, n. 14; Suarez, l. 7 de legibus, c. 19, n. 14.

[6] Const. D. II c. II.

[7] Clem. 2 de aetate.

[8] Pius II. "Cum ex sacrorum."

nor be present therein. Wherefore, in the absence of the dean, the archdeacon, even though not a sub-deacon, can convoke the chapter, propose what is to be done, and receive resolutions, for these things are offices of jurisdiction and not of orders. Likewise in the Order of Friars Preachers a vicar sent from one convent to govern another—passing over for the present the two instances in which he can be sent with active voice—assembles the chapter, gives the necessary instructions, absolves the vocals from excommunication, when necessary, and in fine does everything which pertains to his jurisdiction. A sub-prior will act in like manner, if it chance that he has no voice in the election (Rome, 1601). Finally, one admitted to a chapter of canons by dispensation, is not thereby dispensed to receive sacred orders; hence one so dispensed, does not in virtue of this dispensation acquire active voice in election.[1]

VI. Vocals censured with sentence of excommunication are also deprived of active voice. Excommunication is either major or minor. The latter prohibits the reception of the sacraments, and no longer exists since the publication of the Constitution "Apostolicae Sedis."[2] The former cuts a guilty christian off from the Church and deprives him of its spiritual favors. Those censured with major excommunication are divided into two classes: according as they are to be shunned (vitandi), or tolerated (tolerati), or, in other words, according as they have or have not been formally pronounced excommunicated by the Church.

Those to be shunned cannot take part in elections, and were they knowingly admitted, the election would be ipso facto null and void. Were such a person admitted in good faith, the election would be valid, provided his vote did not decide the election. It would likewise be valid if he could not be expelled without grave danger or scandal. But in this case, the electors must protest before witnesses, publicly, if possible, against his presence, and declare his vote will not be considered.[3] If the electors are not certain that said person has been formally censured, they cannot eject him from the chapter, because in doubt every one must be left in peaceful possession of his rights.

In regard to a tolerated excommunicated person, if no one makes exception to his being present, the election is valid, and cannot be annulled. The vocals commit no fault in admitting him, for they are not obliged to avoid one whom the Church tol-

---

[1] Rota, June 23, 1606.
[2] cf. S. C. S. O. ad IV. Jan. 6, 1884.
[3] Sylvius, electio, n. 17.

erates. Moreover, election being an act of public office, whatever is done by a tolerated excommunicant is sustained by the Church. Wherefore, if all the electors are thus excommunicated, the election is valid, for excommunication does not deprive a person of office or jurisdiction until a formal declaration has been made to this effect. The election is also valid, if conducted by one vocal only, and he a tolerated excommunicant.[1] The same holds if an exception of excommunication is opposed after the election has been concluded. If the exception were interposed prior to the election, the election is voidable. If it is evident, or even doubtful ,that the election was decided by the excommunicant's vote, it must be cassed; but if it is certain that his vote in no way decided the election, said election must be declared valid, and sustained. If, in this hypothesis, particular statutes require unanimous consent for a valid election, one opposing vote of the excommunicant would not invalidate the election, for the candidate would have received the unanimous vote of all the qualified vocals, which alone constitutes a unanimous election.

In the election of a Roman Pontiff excommunication does not nullify, even though every elector be excommunicated.[2] To avoid the danger of schisms in the Church, it was most wisely decreed that exceptions of excommunication cannot be resorted to in papal elections.

In the Order of Friars Preachers no excommunicant should be deprived of active voice, unless he has been pronounced excommunicated by judicial sentence, but an exception may be made against him.[3] The electors can and should eject a notorious excommunicant, if this can be done without scandal, but they are not bound to do so.[4] The excommunicant himself sins in taking part in an election.

VII. Suspension is another censure which deprives a vocal of the right of exercising active voice. It is a censure which deprives a cleric, wholly or partially, of the power of orders, office, or benefice. A person simpliciter suspended is one who is suspended from office and benefice, such a one, therefore, cannot vote in canonical elections. The same is true of him who is suspended from office, for by suspension from office we understand suspension from all clerical exercises. Suspension from one particular office, however, does not prevent one from taking part in

[1] Suarez, sec. 2, n. 3.

[2] Pius IV. "In eligendis"; Greg. XV. "Aeterni Patris"; Pius X. "Vacante Sede Apostolica."

[3] Const. n. 521.

[4] Passerini, Ib. n. 83.

elections. Suspension from a benefice does not deprive an elector of his right to vote, for this species of suspension takes from a person the right of receiving the fruits of a benefice, but in no way interferes with the right of election which is an official act. Suspension from orders does not prevent one from electing, because election is not an act of orders, but of jurisdiction.[1] The discipline given in the preceding section for excommunicants—both tolerated and those to be shunned—obtains also for those in like manner suspended.[2] Neither major nor minor suspension deprives a vocal of the right of suffrage. To sum up only suspension simpliciter from office and from election for a particular reason deprives one of active voice, suspension from a benefice or from orders do not. A suspended vocal sins in exercising active voice, of which he has been deprived.

VIII. Not only excommunication and suspension, but also interdict takes away the right and faculty of voting.[3] And since interdict is an ecclesiastical censure, and the chapter "Ad evitanda" speaks universally of censures, what has been said of excommunication is proportionately understood of interdict, namely that an interdicted elector not formally so declared by judicial sentence, validly exercises suffrage, though he sins in so doing. We shall speak later of election held in interdicted places.

IX. The ninth condition excludes from elections one who has incurred irregularity.[4] Others, however, hold contrary.[5] Both parties base their opinion on a text in the chapter "Is qui," which states that he who celebrates in an interdicted place incurs irregularity, and thereby becomes disqualified and should not be admitted to elections with the others. The negatives apply this doctrine to all species of irregularity, while the affirmatives restrict it to that irregularity alone, which is incurred by celebrating in an interdicted place. We prefer the second opinion, for since irregularity impedes only the execution of orders, and not of jurisdiction, neither does it per se nor consecutively impede the act of electing which is not an act of orders but of jurisdiction. Hence we think it more probable that irregulars can exercise suffrage, except in cases where they have incurred irregularity by celebrating in an interdicted place, or have become infamous, or have been condemned of homicide.[6] In these cases the priva-

[1] Ib. n. 95.
[2] Suarez, V, disp. 26, sect. 2, n. 2; Barbosa I c. 19, n. 23.
[3] Hostiensis, Ib. n. 7; Sylvius, q. 4.
[4] Sylvius, Miranda, Layman, Barbosa, Donatus.
[5] Suarez, Bonacius, Sigismund.
[6] Const. Pius II., Pius V., Sixtus V.

tion of active voice is not by reason of the irregularity, but a penalty annexed.[1] Moreover, even in these cases the irregularity must be formally declared by judicial sentence, before those who have incurred it can be excluded from an election. In the Order of Friars Preachers all who have incurred irregularity in any way are deprived of active voice (Narbonne 1354).

X. In addition to the above requirements, electors must also have all the conditions required by the particular statutes of their various colleges.

In the Order of Friars Preachers several conditions are required by particular statutes for conventual suffrage: 1° Vocals must be assigned to a convent two months previous to the vacancy of the priorship. The two months begins on the day when the assignation is read publicly in the convent ad quem. To elect a socius to a provincial chapter, the vocal must be assigned to the convent two months before said election takes place. This requirement is not necessary: (a) in case of the sudden death of a prior. Likewise, when the office becomes vacant either by the death, removal or resignation of the prior, the subprior acquires active voice, even though he has been assigned to the convent for less than two months; (b) when a vicar has been sent by the provincial to conduct an election. A vicar may be thus sent only in two cases: when there is a great dissension among the vocals, or when their incompetency is such that no one among them knows how to direct the election proceedings; (c) when a lector (primarius vel unicus) has been appointed to take charge of the studium, or when an assignment has been made by the definitors of the provincial chapter; (d) when a vocal who has been prior of another convent, returns to the convent of his former assignment on the expiration of his office; (e) when a vocal two months previous to election is assigned to another convent as prior or for any other office, he retains his voice in the convent a quo until a new prior is elected, confirmed and installed.

2° They must have completed nine years from first profession and have been ordained priests (Avila, 1895). Lay brothers who are transferred to the clerical state, do not acquire active voice until twelve years from the date of transferral (Valladolid, 1605; Rome, 1629).

3° They must have completed their studies, and have received approbation for hearing confessions unless an election occurs within six months from the completion of their studies.

---

[1] Passerini, Ib. n. 105.

4° They cannot by reason of a new assignation vote twice or more in the same year. Neither can they who renounce their vote in one convent elect in another under pretense of a new assignment. Exception is made for regents, lectors, masters of studies, and sub-priors, not however for lectors of cases of conscience.

5° A prior who, during his term of office, is assigned by simple assignation to the convent of which he is prior has no vote in the election of his successor until two months after the expiration of his office. If during his office he be assigned to another convent, he can take no part in the elections of this convent unless he has served the convent in good faith for two months after the completion of his priorship.

6° Before brothers of one province can vote in another they must have been assigned for a year, or at least the greater part of a year in the province in which the election is to take place. There are two exceptions to this discipline: the first is when a brother of one province is affiliated to another, he immediately acquires active voice, provided he has the other requisites of common law and particular statute. The second case is when brothers go from Spain to the Indies, if eligible by law, they acquire voice as soon as they shall have reached those provinces (Rome, 1589).

7° Vocals must not remain outside the cloister, for those dwelling outside the cloister under any pretext whatsoever—even with permission of superiors, lose active and passive voice. Therefore, those raised to dignities outside the order, or who have received benefices, no longer enjoy suffrage. This must be understood of secular benefices, not of those united to the order. Hence pastors of churches connected with the order are not considered outside the cloister while in their parishes by the obedience of superiors.[1] But chaplains of secular churches and of other orders, provided they remain outside the cloister day and night, confessors of nuns, kings, and princes, theologians of bishops and cardinals, and all others outside the obedience of the order, even with permission of superiors, can neither elect nor be elected (Rome, 1601). Those who remain outside the order without the consent of superiors cannot exercise passive voice until ten years after their return (Rome, 1525).

Those who for any reason, except for the office of Sacred Inquisition, permanently remain outside their convents for more than six months immediately previous to an election, cannot

[1] Camillus, c. 5, n. 8.

exercise active voice therein. Likewise, those who ordinarily dwell outside, v. g., in a vicariate erected with apostolic authority, are not admitted to conventual elections (Lyons, 1891; Vienna, 1898).

The Chapter of Rome (1553) declared that the master general could dispense from the laws regarding the exercise of voice by one outside the cloister. But a difficulty here arises, for the law concerning secular benefices is not a constitution of the order, but a decree of Sixtus IV (1478). And since a general cannot dispense in papal legislation, we think that the general cannot admit to voice a vocal holding a secular benefice, unless he renounce it—although he can dispense him from remaining in the convent.[1]

XI. Electors cannot vote in elections, if they have been deprived of voice. But they should not be excluded before they have been declared deprived by judicial sentence.[2] In the Order of Friars Preachers this declaration must be made one month before the time of an election, or when in the congregation of vocals one is found to lack the conditions required for exercise of voice.

One juridically deprived of voice should be excluded from the chapter even with force, if necessary, except when he makes a legitimate appeal, which suspends the sentence and its effect. The discipline concerning those deprived of voice but tolerated and those to be shunned, and likewise that of interposing exceptions is the same as that given above for excommunicated vocals.

XII. All who have been branded as infamous are excluded from election. Infamy is the loss of reputation, and arises either from law or from fact. Infamy of fact does not destroy the faculty of voting, for it very frequently is occasioned by ignorance, sarcasm, imprudence, or hatred; neither does it prevent one from being a scrutineer. Those branded with infamy of law cannot elect, for election is a legitimate act, and since legitimate acts are prohibited to the infamous, it follows that one thus branded cannot elect. Infamy of either kind is not incurred before juridical sentence has been given to this effect. Hence before he has been juridically declared infamous, an elector can validly take part in elections, and does not sin in so doing.

[1] Passerini, Ib. n. 124.
[2] Ib. n. 135.

CHAPTER IV

Convocation of Electors

Having established the efficient cause of election in the preceding chapter, we shall now offer a consideration of its formal cause. And since election pertains per se primo to a college, its formal cause consists in the collegiate congregation of those electors who compose the college. To bring this about, the electors must be summoned. Hence a treatment of the formal cause of election is an exposition of the doctrine regarding the convocation of electors, to which this present chapter will be devoted.

We cannot lay down a particular rule for the convocation of electors, for this depends upon the diversity of elections and colleges, their respective rights and customs. Wherefore, the general rule is that the electors should be convoked by the one upon whom this office is imposed by law or custom. If there be no such law or custom, then the duty falls to him who is oldest in office, unless there be another of greater dignity, in which case the latter summons the electors.

In the Order of Friars Preachers the sub-prior ordinarily convokes the electors. If a convent is without a superior, the three capitulars oldest by profession elect a vicar, who convokes a chapter for the election of a prior, unless other provision be made by higher superiors.[1] If the sub-prior, whose duty it is to assemble the electors three or four days after the vacancy of the priorship, or the vicar, if there be no subprior, refuse to call the chapter at the request of the majority of the vocals, the oldest vocal may do so, and he unwilling, then the next oldest in religion, and so on until the election is begun.[2]

The convocation of electors is an act of jurisdiction, hence it always pertains to him who is the head or superior of the community, even though he may have no voice in the election. In the elections of conventual priors, or of socii to provincial chapters, the superior is the sub-prior, or he being absent, the vicar, unless the provincial or general appoints a special vicar to preside at the election. The superior of a provincial election is the

---

[1] Const. D. II. C. II.

[2] Const. n. 548.

vicar of the province, but in the election of definitors of a provincial chapter, either the provincial himself or more commonly the vicar of the province presides. If the provincial is not present at the election of definitors of a general chapter, the presiding vicar takes charge. When an election of a master general occurs, the vicar of the order, even though not a vocal, is the presiding prelate. Conventual priors cannot convoke a chapter for the election of a socius, for special law forbids the prior to take part in such elections.

Those vocals should be called to election qui debent, volunt, et possunt commode interesse.[1] Therefore all those—whether present or absent—who have the right to elect should be summoned. If there is a custom of not calling the absent, it should be observed.[2] A period of ten years suffices for such a custom to obtain.[3] He who is in possession of election, even though his right be not a true one, validly elects and should be called, for the right of election follows possession. But mere possession with common error will not suffice, there is further required a colored title conferred by a competent superior.[4] Exceptions made after election against such a vocal are of no moment, even though his defects are made manifest, for at the time of the election he was in peaceful possession by a common error and colored title. For outsiders, however, possession, good faith, and colored title are not sufficient, unless the possession were lawfully prescribed by an existing custom. We shall return to this point on a later page, where we shall explain more in detail who are and who are not to be called in certain cases.

Every vocal is obliged to vote, and is therefore obliged to be present at elections, for this obligation—supposing the institution of election—is based on natural law. A person possessing a faculty necessary to the common good is bound to exercise that faculty. This obligation does not bind per se under pain of mortal sin or even venial; it could bind either way, or it could accidentally cease. Hence the gravity of the obligation is to be reckoned in proportion to its necessity to the common good. If, for example, a heretic were to be elected bishop, an elector is bound —whether the outcome be doubtful or certain—to do all in his power to prevent the election, even at the risk of his life.[5]

[1] cap. Quia propter.

[2] Sylvius, electio I, n. 6, d. 2.

[3] Miranda, q. 26, n .6; Barbosa, I, c. 19, n. 89.

[4] Cajetan, confessionis iteratio; Sylvius, Confessor 1 q. 19.

[5] Passerini, Ib. c. 11, n. 22.

If an elector is in doubt as to whom he should elect, Sylvius maintains he is not bound to vote at all.[1] We prefer the opposite opinion, for the renunciation of a vote very frequently favors the election of an unworthy candidate. Should he consider his right to vote doubtful, he may renounce it. But if he is certain of his right, he is bound to vote for the one he considers the most worthy, for by renunciation, he at least exposes himself to the danger of favoring an evil and unjust election. Under renunciation of voice comes also the casting of blank votes, for these votes are not computed, but subtracted from the whole number, and therefore affect the election, and could further the election of an unworthy candidate. Electors are therefore forbidden to cast such votes, unless they are certain that by so doing, no injury will accrue to the community.

The above principles are indeed true and should be adhered to, still in practice it generally makes slight difference to the community if one or two electors absent themselves from an election. Hence renunciation of voice is not of its nature a mortal sin, because it is not per se a grave injury to the community were one of the electors to neglect his duty. Even the negligence of the whole chapter is not per se a mortal sin, for it is not strictly speaking a grave injury to the community, because in such a case the election would devolve by law to the superior. And since a prelacy is often better provided for by the institution of a superior than by the election of a college, good could follow from the neglect of a chapter to vote. But all things considered, it is much better and safer for every elector to exercise his right, because his not doing so could easily injure the common good, and thus constitute a mortal sin were the injury of a serious nature.

The chapter "Quia propter" says that those should be summoned to an election, who wish (qui volunt) to take part therein. This does not hold when the interest of the Church demands their presence, for the good of the Church preponderates that of electors. The superior of the election, therefore, the public good demanding, can compel an elector to come to an election, and to cast a vote de se useful, for to cast a blank vote is not to elect, but to renounce one's voice.[2]

The decree also states that those must be called who can conveniently present themselves (qui possunt commode interesse). It is important to note that the word conveniently refers not to the convenience of the electors, but rather to that of

[1] Electio 2. n. 15.

[2] Ib. n. 23

the Church.[1] Wherefore, when the necessity of holding an election is so imminent that there is no time to call the electors, or when war, pestilence and the like prevents their being called, or when by calling them serious injury would fall upon the Church, no summons should be sent to them, notwithstanding any custom to the contrary.[2] For when a grave injury threatens the Church, the custom of calling electors must not be observed. Cases of doubt are to be settled by the superior of the election, but to avoid subsequent difficulties he should consult the electors present, and if possible the superior upon whom the confirmation of the election depends.[3]

Even though all the electors could be called without grave injury to the Church, still it is not necessary to call those who are at too great a distance.[4] The Gloss holds that all who are in the diocese or province must be called. We hesitate to accept this principle, for it can easily happen that a vocal, though within the confines of a province, is nevertheless at a great distance from the place of election, while another outside the province is near at hand. It seems, then, we should rather consider whether or not the absent vocal can be conveniently summoned. Special laws determining the distances must be observed. In the Order of Friars Preachers those vocals must be called who are not distant more than one day's journey by ordinary means of travel.[5] The law makes no provision for travel by aeroplane.

Absent vocals whose whereabouts are known, should if convenient be called personally, unless custom ordain otherwise. The citation should be made by letter or messenger, and for a certain day. If the vocal does not arrive at the accustomed hour for holding the election, the other electors may proceed at once with the election. If his whereabouts are unknown the summons should be left at his home; if he has no fixed residence, then the citation should be made by a public edict on the doors of the church, which is situated in a place where he usually stops, or it should be read publicly in the chapter. Finally, if his whereabouts and accustomed place of dwelling are both unknown, and diligent inquiry has been made, the summons is to be fastened on the doors of the place in which the election is to be held, or to be read in the chapter or at the public table.

---

[1] cap. "Quod sicut," 28 de electione.

[2] cap. "Ecclesiarum," dist. 11.

[3] Passerini, Ib., n. 33.

[4] cap. "Cum inter" 8, Ib.

[5] Avila, 1895.

Those present should be summoned orally or by the sound of a bell, but the electors must be previously advised that this bell is a summons to the election chamber. In some institutes, as in the Order of Friars Preachers, the hour appointed for the election is announced either in the refectory or in some other public manner on the day previous; where this custom prevails individual intimation is unnecessary. If after a convenient time from the ringing of the bell the capitulars do not present themselves, or if they are not at hand at the time appointed, the other vocals may proceed without them, though it is better to notify them that the chapter is awaiting their arrival. Should all the electors be congregated in the same place, they may, if they wish, proceed with the election, citation in such a case being unnecessary.

If on the appointed day the election is postponed for a definite future time, the electors—even the absent—need not be resummoned. But if it is postponed indefinitely a second citation must be sent to all. Should the person elected refuse his consent, a resummons is not required, for every elector should know that another election is to take place as soon as possible. Although one citation is sufficient, still if the time and place appointed be changed, the vocals should be notified. When a time and place are fixed by law or custom, no intimation is needed, provided that the vocals know that the office is vacant.[1]

The superior of the election, not of himself but with the consent of the majority of the electors, can abbreviate the time fixed by law, and the day once having been fixed, the superior must be present thereon, otherwise the vocals may hold the election without him. In like manner the majority of the capitulars can restrict the prescribed time, and compel the superior to conform, if he can give no just reason for not doing so; but for a sufficient reason he can prevent this anticipation and defer the election to the lawful time. And since the law concedes to the superior the right of determining the day within the time allotted for election, his judgment—if reasonable—must be accepted by the electors, and only in the last hour of the prescribed time—which passing, the election would devolve to higher authority—can the electors proceed without him. In the Order of Friars Preachers it is decreed that after the third or fourth day from the notification of the vacancy of the priorship, the majority of vocals can compel the superior of the election to convene the chapter, and if he refuse, they may proceed without him.[2]

[1] Panormitanus, n. 8, de electione.
[2] Const. n. 548.

Electors who are disqualified according to natural law should not be summoned. Those who have been juridically declared unqualified must not be called, but rather expelled if they present themselves. But vocals—no matter however notorious a crime they may have committed—who will be deprived of voice only by a condemnatory sentence (ferendae sentiae), should be cited, for they still have the right to vote, and should any one protest, the protestation is not to be heeded. But if the privation is to be imposed by a declaratory sentence (latae sententiae), they should not be called, and actions for annulment are not admitted, for no injury was done by not calling them, since they will be judged to have been deprived of voice at the time of election.[1] He alone, therefore, whose inhability is so occult that he cannot be convicted thereof, can enter a complaint (exceptio de contemptu) if he is not called.

Note here that it is one thing to expel a vocal, and another not to call him. The first takes away the possession of voice, so when inhability requires judicial sentence, it is not lawful to expel a disqualified vocal by private authority. Not to call a vocal does not deprive him of his possession, but merely signifies he has no voice. No injury is therefore done in the latter case, for since he has already been deprived of voice by law, he has forfeited the right to be cited, although he still retains the right not to be expelled and deprived of his possession. For if such a person has a right that his possession be not taken from him, he has not for that reason a right that there be given to him something he does not possess.[2] To avoid subsequent trouble it would be better to call him, and admit him under protestation. But the electors are not bound to await his arrival—even though called, and he cannot enter a complain, because he has no right to suffrage. Some hold he can bring suit for expenses contracted, because the summons was an occasion of loss to him.[3]

Should an elector renounce his his voice, and afterwards regret his having done so, he may reclaim it, and should be cited and admitted to the election, otherwise he can bring action against it. Affairs transacted in the meantime are valid, but he must have part in those that follow. For active voice is conceded for the public good, and one renouncing something pertaining to the public good always has the obligation of reassuming it.

If absent vocals—sufficient time having been given—do not come to the chapter at the appointed time, they are presumed to

---

[1] Innoc. c. Cum Vintonien; Sylvius Ib. n. 1; Barbosa, c. 2, de post. n. 4.

[2] Sigismund, d. 10, n. 5.

[3] Hostiensis, Panormitanus.

have alienated themselves from the electoral body, but if they arrive before the completion of the election, they must be admitted to a part in the business which still remains to be transacted. Those departing from an assembled chapter at the time fixed for election are also presumed to have renounced their voice, and if by waiting their return the election would devolve to the superior, the remaining electors—whether they be many, few or even one—can validly elect, and the departed cannot institute annulment proceedings.[1] Even in the election of a Roman Pontiff, if but one cardinal from those cited remain, he can hold the election.[2] When the allotted time has not expired, a vocal for a just reason may appeal for an extension, and the other electors even though present in large numbers cannot elect, otherwise he who appealed may bring suit against their action, and at his instance the election is cassed. But no appeal can be made, if the time allowed is about to expire.

In the Order of Friars Preachers those who do not respond to the summons forfeit their right to vote. If, however, after the capitulars assemble, the majority should depart, the minority cannot proceed with the election until the full time granted by the constitutions has expired. Should the majority of those assembled disapprove of the time and place appointed by the superior, and depart from the chapter, the proceedings must be suspended; if they give approval they may recall their consent at any time before the conclusion of election, even though the scrutineers have already begun to collect the ballots. Although the majority has not the right to neglect the citation, still it has the right of not electing, if it seems good to them to defer the election.[3]

When all the vocals who have a right to be called to an election are not called, a valid election requires an absolute majority —or even two-thirds where law or custom demands—not of those present, but of those both present and absent. Thus if there were but twenty present of the thirty who have a right to be present, the others having been contemned, it is not sufficient for the elect to obtain eleven or even fifteen votes, but to be elected validly he must receive sixteen, or where a majority of two-thirds is required, twenty must be cast for him. Where the one elected was nominated by the majority of the thirty the election is valid in substance, but each of those contemned has the right to file an exception against it. If one or more of those

[1] Passerini, Ib. n. 93.

[2] Ib.

[3] Glossa, Const. D. II. C. II.

contemned arrive after the scrutiny has been announced, but before the publication of the election in the name of the college, a new scrutiny must be taken, but the other transactions should not be repeated. If one contemned arrive after the election has been concluded, the chapter cannot resort to a fresh scrutiny. An election does not by reason of vocals having been contemned devolve to a superior, but it pertains to the same electors with the addition of those previously contemned.

The fact that one or more of the vocals are contemned does not, according to canon law, render an election void, but it is voidable at the instance of the person or persons contemned. Although an election is invalid if the majority of the electors were contemned, because—as shown above—the candidate in such a case cannot obtain a majority of necessary votes, it is not, however, invalid for the reason that the vocals were contemned, for the calling of vocals does not belong to the substance of election, but its omission is unjust, because it is injurious and contrary to their rights. No prelate inferior to the Holy Father nor general chapter can make a law declaring ipso facto null an election, in which one or more vocals were contemned.[1] But an election to which all have not been summoned is not voidable at the instance of any one other than those contemned, for the injury is personal and it therefore pertains to that person or persons to enter an action for annulment or to consider the election lawful.[2]

Annulment proceedings must be filed before the confirmation or institution of the candidate, unless it is manifest that the contemned vocal was unaware of the election and confirmation, in which case the action should be admitted even after the confirmation or institution. If he should die during the proceedings, his successor may or may not continue the case.[3] The burden of proof lies with the electors and not with the one contemned, because the presumption is that the latter would not have neglected to exercise his right. The oath of a messenger is sufficient proof.[4] If the superior of the election cited the absentee in the ordinary way by letter or messenger, but for one reason or another he did not receive the message, he cannot institute annulment proceedings, provided it is evident that the superior in good faith did what he could to notify the absent vocal, for in this case he was not contemned by the superior or electors. But if before the

[1] Rota in Toletana Canonicatus, 18 Maii, 1584.
[2] Passerini, Ib. n. 120.
[3] Samuel, n. 2.
[4] Glossa in cap. Quod sicut.

election it becomes known that he was not called, and there is time to defer the election, it must be deferred until he is notified and has had sufficient time to reach the place of election.[1]

The right of religious to enter suit for annulment is sharply controverted. If a superior acts as judge, we think he cannot forbid an elector to make an exception, because it is a right conceded by law to all ecclesiastics, and confirmed by common custom; hence regular superiors cannot deny such concessions to their subjects. But if he acts as a prelate in virtue of the dominion, which is his from the vow of obedience, he can for a just reason forbid his subject to file a complaint, because a subject is bound to obey the precepts of a superior, and to sacrifice his own interest for the common good.[2]

---

[1] Passerini, Ib. n. 129.

[2] Samuel, Sigismund, Passerini Ib.

CHAPTER V

Persons Eligible

The material cause of canonical election is the persons eligible for ecclesiastical offices or benefices. Those persons are eligible who meet the requirements of natural and ecclesiastical law, and also of the particular statutes relating to the office to be provided. Our paper will be restricted to a consideration of those qualifications demanded by common ecclesiastical law, since a treatment of those exacted by particular laws pertains to the various institutes whose statutes require them.

I. Natural law requires a candidate to be in full possession of his reason, without which no one is capable of directing himself or others to their final end.[1] Hence infants and the insane are excluded. Those who once suffered from insanity, even if restored, are nevertheless still ineligible by positive law until they obtain papal dispensation.[2] The election of such a person is not only illicit, but ipso jure null. Habitual drunkards are also ineligible because they are accustomed to deprive themselves of the use of reason. Demoniacs,—officially so declared—owing to their defective liberty and weakness of mind, are likewise excluded, but if freed from their infirmity, they become eligible—their restoration, however, cannot be presumed but must be proved. For proof one year of health is regularly sufficient, and even then if any one makes opposition, a declaration of the bishop is necessary. Epilectics are irregular and ineligible, but those rarely subject to this infirmity are eligible. A lapse of thirty days since a previous attack suffices to establish one's recovery.[3]

II. No person is eligible for an ecclesiastical office unless he is possessed of such knowledge as is required for a prudent administration of the office.[4] The Council of Trent[5] decreed that no one could be elected to office who was not acquainted with the rudiments of faith and did not know how to read and write. Positive law requires that all those promoted to ecclesiastical benefices have a knowledge of the latin tongue. Bishops must

[1] S. Thos. la 2ae. q. 1, art. 1.
[2] Rodrig. II, q. 54, a. 5; Passerini C. 25, n. 6.
[3] Turrecrem. I q. 2, c. 2.
[4] S. Thos. la 2ae q. 76, art. 2.
[5] Sess. 23, c. 4.

have an adequate knowledge of all the sacred sciences, and undergo a diligent examination therein; they should be masters, doctors, or licentiates in sacred theology or canon law.[1] At least one half of the dignities in cathedral churches should be conferred only on masters or doctors in theology, or licentiates in canon law.[2] Pastors must know how to distinguish sins, to explain the gospel and sacraments. Regular prelates are not required to have that knowledge which bishops must possess. In the Order of Friars Preachers a prior must be able to expound the word of God and to speak latin.[3]

Dispensations from defects of knowledge required by natural or supernatural law cannot be obtained. The Supreme Pontiff alone can dispense from that required by ecclesiastical law, and only when there is a well-founded hope that the necessary knowledge will be acquired within a short time. A bishop for a good reason may confer a benefice on one of inadequate knowledge, provided that he himself administer the benefice until the one appointed acquires sufficient knowledge.[4]

III. The nature of election in general requires the elect to be a human being endowed with free use of reason, and possessed of a knowledge necessary for the prudent exercise of the office to which he has been elected. These conditions supposed, we now logically pass to the treatment of those which pertain to ecclesiastical elections in particular, the first and foremost of which is faith, for faith is the foundation of the whole ecclesiastical hierarchy. Those who are wanting in faith are either they who have never been baptized, or they who baptized have afterwards lost the faith.

Persons not baptized are ineligible to all ecclesiastical functions. For not being members of the Church, they are incapable of ecclesiastical jurisdiction and administration, and hence if elected to an ecclesiastical office, such election would be invalid by divine law. Conversion to the faith, however, renders them and their baptized descendents eligible. Special legislation of some religious institutes exclude the descendents of Jews and Saracens from all dignities. Clement VIII ordained that in the kingdom of Portugal descendants of Hebrews to the seventh generation were ineligible to all cathedral dignities, the principal collegiate dignities, parishes and benefices. Neophytes, or adults

[1] ib. sess. 7, c. 1, de ref.

[2] ib.

[3] Const. N. 507.

[4] Palaus N. 12.

recently baptized, are also ineligible. The length of time in which they remain in the class of neophytes is left to the judgment of the bishop, and during that time he can for no consideration grant a dispensation from the irregularity under which they labor.[1] Catechumens are for a greater reason ineligible. But children of neophytes and catechumens baptized before the use of reason are eligible.

The election of a heretic, according to canon law, is null and void. It can be validly confirmed by the Pope, but the confirmation strictly speaking is illicit.[2] Those also who defend, favour or harbour heretics, together with their children to the second generation, are ineligible.[3] But a child is not to be deprived of a benefice obtained before his father's relapse into heresy. Schismatics, if at the same time heretics, being subject to all the penalties of heretics, are therefore ineligible. The same is true of schismatics who are not heretics, and they remain ineligible even if they repent and become reconciled to the Church. If the schism be public, the pope alone can dispense; if occult, bishops can dispense by virtue of indult from the Council of Trent.[4]

IV. Persons not born in lawful wedlock are ineligible to all ecclesiastical orders, dignities or beneficies, unless legitimized by subsequent marriage, or by dispensation for the reception of orders. Even though legitimized in either of these two ways, an illegitimate to receive the dignity of the cardinalate must obtain a special dispensation.[5] The children of invalid marriages contracted in good faith are considered legitimate. Illegitimate religious are eligible for the reception and administration of orders, but not for prelacies or dignities, and neither do they become so by religious profession except through dispensation. Common law excludes them from prelacies alone, but particular laws of the different institutes exclude them from many other offices. In the Order of Friars Preachers they are barred from offices of prior, sub-prior, vicar, definitor, preacher general, and master of theology.[6] In the Order of Friars Minor they cannot be chosen general, provincial, guardian, custos, conventual vicar, definitor, procurator to provincial or general chapters, discreet, commissary, visitor, but they may act as novice-master or confessor of

[1] Sanchez II, c. 28, n. 11.
[2] Passerini ib. n. 68.
[3] cap. Quicumque—de haereticis in VI.
[4] Sanchez, Barbosa, Garzias.
[5] cap. Cum in cunctis.
[6] Passerini ib. n. 157.

nuns, provided there be no external jurisdiction annexed to the office.

The Holy Father alone can grant dispensations for the promotion of illegitimates to sacred orders, dignities, and prelacies. Bishops have faculties to grant like dispensations for the reception of minor orders and benefices not having the care of souls. Religious superiors by special provileges can dispense their illegitimate subjects from ineligibility to prelacies. In the Order of Friars Preachers only the general may grant these dispensations. The pope dispenses for the office of general in religious orders. Dispensations granted without a just cause by any superior except the pope are invalid;[1] if granted by the pope, they are indeed valid, but he sins in granting them.[2] It is difficult to say exactly what would constitute a just cause. Very many are given by authors, such as public good, avoidance of scandal, knowledge, good works, necessity, and the like. If vocals knowingly elect an illegitimate they commit a grave sin and should be severely punished, and the person freely accepting the prelacy sins mortally since he violates a precept of the sacred canons. The promotion, however, is valid, but he is held to renounce it or to obtain a dispensation; if he cannot do either without loss of reputation to himself or his relatives, he may retain it.[3]

V. In the fifth place health and strength of body are required for eligibility to office. Hence the blind, deaf, or dumb, those suffering from a notable defect in sight, hearing or speech, those whom infirmity prevents from performing the principal duties of an office, those inordinately given to laziness, sleeping or eating, those noticeably deformed or mutilated by absence of fingers, hands or feet are unqualified. In the Order of Friars Preachers, he who is unable to attend to choral and other community exercises cannot be elected prior.

The election of an infirm person is not ipso jure null, for we can find no legislation to this effect. If he is morally certain that his infirmity is such as will impede him in the exercise of his office, the elect is bound to refuse his consent, and to do all in his power to prevent confirmation.[4] But if certainty is wanting, he may validly and lawfully accept the office. If after confirmation infirmity should render him incompetent, he cannot be removed from office, but a coadjutor must be given to him. In the

---

[1] cap. Cuncta 9, q. 3.

[2] Cajetan, dispensatio II. q. 96, a. 5.

[3] Rodrig. t. 1, q. 13, a. 5.

[4] Passerini ib. n. 331.

Order of Friars Preachers, generals cannot be removed by a general chapter on account of infirmity, for generals can be removed only for those reasons given in the Constitutions, among which infirmity is not mentioned, but they can be urged to resign by the definitors of the general chapter, if the latter judge such resignation to be expedient.

VI. Incorporation into the ecclesiastical state is required before a person becomes eligible for canonical charges or functions. Those elected to benefices must have at least first tonsure, otherwise the election is ipso facto null.[1] The presentation of a layman to a benefice is also null, unless he become a cleric before the time appointed for conferring the benefice. Although Saints Nicolas, Severus and Ambrose were elected to the episcopacy from the laity, still these elections were by a special inspiration of the Holy Ghost. It is not necessary to be in orders at the time of one's having been elected, but the elect must be qualified to receive the required orders within the time established by law.

Religious superiors have power either of jurisdiction or dominion, or both. Since jurisdiction is not per se required in a superior, but dominion suffices, it follows that the clerical state is not per se necessary. This is clear from the fact that abbesses, though not enjoying jurisdiction, have the power of governing. Likewise the early obbots, though not clerics, were superiors.

Superiors of religious communities must be professed in their respective community, otherwise their elections are invalid.[2] The pope alone can confer abbeys and benefices requiring administration on those not professed. This being penal discipline, is not extended to collation or postulation. Nuns cannot be elected abbesses or prioresses before they have completed eight or at least five years from profession.[3] In religious orders of men, common law ordains that one may be elected immediately after profession, provided he meet all the other requirements. In the Order of Friars Preachers no religious is eligible before he has passed twelve complete years from profession.[4]

For election to the episcopate one must have been in sacred orders for six months.[5] Hence a sub-deacon may be elected bishop. But an election of one not in sacred orders is not de jure invalid, for in ancient times members of the laity were elected

[1] Sixtus V. Const. Sacrosanctum.

[2] Conc. Trid. sess. 14, c. 10 de ref.

[3] ib. sess. 25, c. 7 de regular.

[4] Valencia 1596; Naples 1600.

[5] Conc. Trid. sess. 22, c. 2.

bishops in cases of necessity, and history tells us that Saint Ambrose while still a catechumen was raised to the episcopate. But since priesthood is required under pain of nullity before a bishop can be consecrated, a bishop-elect must be ordained priest shortly after his confirmation, for he must receive consecration within three months from the date of confirmation under penalty of losing the fruits of his see, and should he neglect it for another three months he forfeits the see itself.[1]

Religious superiors must have received tonsure at least. Beneficiaries who are not ordained priests within a year of their having taken possession of a benefice, ipso facto lost it. Deans of colleges, priors, and conventual abbots are excepted from this general assertion, since in such institutions there are priests by whom the care of souls can be exercised. Here, as elsewhere, the particular statutes of each order must be considered. In order to possess passive voice in the Order of Friars Preachers, one must be an approved confessor; hence ordination to the priesthood is also required.

VII. The seventh condition requires a suitable age in the person to be elected. The age of seven years suffices to obtain a simple benefice, if the founder expressly so declare.[2] The Council of Trent laid down some general rules on this point: 1° no one, even having first tonsure and minor orders, can obtain a benefice before the beginning of his fourteenth year; 2° no one can accept an ecclesiastical dignity, unless he be of such an age as to receive the required order within the lawfully prescribed time. The age of twenty-one complete years is required for the subdiaconate, twenty-two for the diaconate, and twenty-four for the priesthood. Fourteen years suffices for a canonry, to which the care of souls is not annexed. 3° clerics of twenty-two years may be elected to cathedral dignities, not having the care of souls. The canon penitentiary must be forty years of age, but if no one in the diocese meets this requirement, the bishop may choose the one best qualified. This law also applies to collegiate churches. 4° to be promoted to a dignity having the care of souls, one must be twenty-five years of age, unless the care of souls is committed to a vicar. 5° bishops must have completed thirty years, cardinal deacons twenty-two, cardinal priests and bishops thirty. A cardinal deacon must have been a cleric in minor orders for at least one year, and must receive the diaconate within a year from his elevation. A cardinal priest must be a sub-deacon at the time of his elevation, and immediately be ordained priest.

[1] ib. sess. 23, c. 2.
[2] Barbosa in Conc. trid. sess. 23, c. 6, n. 1.

Religious generals, provincials and abbots must be twenty-five years of age. Conventual priors must have completed twenty-four years, unless the care of souls is exercised by secular priests, in which case twenty years suffice. Abbesses and prioresses should be not less than forty years. Definitors having the care of souls must be twenty-five years of age, but for electors of generals or provincials, the age required for profession suffices. In the Order of Friars Preachers since no one acquires passive voice before the completion of twelve years from profession, and since no one is professed until he has completed his sixteenth year, it follows that no one is eligible before completing his twenty-eighth year. Some provinces have special statutes in this regard.

The pope alone can dispense from the age required by the sacred canons. Ordinaries may dispense in virtue of apostolic indult, which is sometimes granted them. Other elections of those not having the required age are not void but voidable. Dispensations for the reception of orders are rarely granted except for priesthood. Bishops in virtue of indult may grant a dispensation for six months, the Sacred Congregation of Sacraments for twenty months, the Holy Father for twenty-one months.

Advanced age that renders one incapable of exercising an office renders one ineligible for such an office.[1] Canon law fixes no age limit, hence this matter rests with the judgment of superiors.

VIII. Excommunicated persons are ineligible to all ecclesiastical benefices, for the election, postulation, presentation or collation of an excommunicate, even by the motu proprio of the Roman Pontiff, is ipso facto invalid.[2] This is true even though both electors and elect are unconscious of the excommunication. The election of one unjustly though juridically excommunicated is also invalid, but if unjustly inflicted, the election is valid. Should the censure be pardoned before the confirmation, the election still remains invalid, for what was invalid in the beginning cannot be validated; in this case the confirmation would also be invalid. If an invalid election could be made valid, the confirmation would likewise be valid. When the pope confers a prelacy on an excommunicate, the election is valid, because it is presumed that he previously absolved from the censure.

Persons absolved from excommunication may with dispensation retain their benefice or prelacy, which dispensation can be

[1] S. Thos. 2a 2ae, q. 185, art. 4.
[2] Cap. Postulastis.

given only by him who can confer the benefice independently of a third party. Wherefore a bishop cannot dispense: a) when the collation of a benefice pertains to an inferior—unless he consent; b) when the benefice was conferred by the pope; c) when a third has the right of presenting a candidate. Those who knowingly elect or present an excommunicate to an office are by law deprived of voice. Subsequent excommunication does not invalidate an election.

IX. Absolute suspension from office or from a benefice excludes promotion to ecclesiastical dignities. One suspended from office, though not suspended from his benefice, is ineligible to acquire a new benefice.[1] Suspension from orders includes ineligibility to benefices requiring the use of orders, but not from simple benefices. Suspension from one order does not mean ineligibility to a benefice that does not require the use of that order.[2] A person suspended from a benefice may be elected to an office which is not a benefice, and a person suspended from a benefice in one church may be elected to one in another. But absolute suspension from benefices renders one ineligible for election to an office. The election of one simpliciter suspended from a benefice or an office, is ipso jure void. Suspension from an office does not render election to a new benefice void, but rather voidable.[3]

X. Persons under interdict are unqualified for the exercise of passive voice. Whoever violates a local or personal interdict becomes irregular, and therefore ineligible for benefices and prelacies. But he who unconsciously and in good faith violates an interdict is not irregular nor ineligible for office. The election of one violating an interdict is ipso jure null and void.[4]

XI. Another impediment that renders the reception of ecclesiastical charges voidable is irregularity. We have no express text to this effect, but we can easily deduce it from other texts. For whoever is excluded from one thing is likewise barred from everything connected with it. But irregularity prohibits the reception and exercise of sacred orders, to which benefices are annexed. It follows therefore that irregulars are ineligible for ecclesiastical offices or benefices. All benefices do not suppose sacred orders, still they do not admit a canonical impediment to the reception and administration of orders. Irregularity incurred

---

[1] Sanchez II, c. 2, dub. 15.

[2] Passerini ib. n. 489.

[3] Suarez. disp. 28, sec. 3, n. 81.

[4] Ib. n. 16.

without culpability after the reception of an order is not an impediment to promotion to a benefice not requiring the exercise of the prohibited order.[1] So also irregularity impeding episcopal consecration is not an impediment for election to a religious prelacy.[2]

Although the common opinion of canonists is that the election of an irregular is ipso pure null and void, we prefer the contrary, for there is no text expressly stating that it is ipso jure null. From the principle: "whoever is forbidden to exercise the acts of an office, is likewise forbidden to be elected to that office," we cannot deduce that such an election is ipso facto void, but rather that it is voidable. Nor can it be said that because the law prohibits the conferring of a benefice on an irregular, such a collation would be ipso jure null and void. This latter opinion is held by many authors of note, among whom are Innocent III,[3] Sylvius,[4] Suarez.[5] And in its favor is the fact that the pope in conferring benefices does not dispense from irregularity, as he does from censures, which proves that if irregularity rendered the collation of a benefice ipso facto null, he would dispense from it.[6]

Hence it follows that an irregular is not bound in conscience to lay aside a benefice, and to retain it validly he needs only to obtain a dispensation from the irregularity, which dispensation he must in conscience seek as soon as possible. If the matter is brought to the external forum, he should be deprived of his benefice. In freely accepting a benefice, an irregular sins, being disobedient to the sacred canons in a serious matter.[7]

Irregulars may be elected discreets, electors of a general or provincial, socii or definitors to general and provincial chapters, for these offices require jurisdiction in the external forum only, and do not flow from the power of orders, nor are they ordained to it. Irregularity does not impede the power of jurisdiction, nor its use. In a certain sense these offices could be called benefices, still they do not per se or from their nature suppose orders, nor are they ordained to them, as are simple benefices, which are previous dispositions to orders.[8]

---

[1] Passerini ib. n. 507.

[2] Suarez. IV de Relig. t. 8, l. 2, c. 4, n. 25.

[3] Cap. 6 de praeb.

[4] Excommunicato 4, n. 4.

[5] ib. sec. 2, n. 35.

[6] Passerini ib. n. 517.

[7] ib.

[8] Sigismund ib. dub. 67, n. 3; Passerini ib. n. 520.

XII. Since honesty of morals is required for promotion to benefices and prelacies, the brand of infamy renders a person ineligible to these offices.[1]

Infamy of fact, which is based on the rational and probable conjectures of a number of reliable persons, impedes the worthy acquisition of ecclesiastical charges, but does not render canonical elections or collations null and void. For iniquitous persons are not even by natural law incapable of jurisdiction, power or dominion; on the contrary Christ Himself said of the wicked Pharisees: "The Scribes and Pharisees have sitten on the chair of Moses. All things therefore whatsoever they shall say to you, observe and do; but according to their works do ye not."[2] In such elections all parties concerned sin grievously, but the election, confirmation, or collation is not by reason of the infamy invalid, except when the pain of nullity is ipso jure imposed by a particular statute. No one properly speaking can dispense from infamy of fact; it is removed only by penance. Bishops and religious prelates can declare whether it is infamy or rumor, whether it is still present or has been wiped out by penance.[3]

Infamy of law, which by a decree of law brands a person as infamous, deprives one of legal repute, that is, of one's right to good repute. This is the primary effect, and from this proceeds a secondary effect, which is ineligibility to legitimate acts. Despite many opinions to the contrary, it seems certain that the moment a crime is committed, infamy of law takes away the right to, but not the possession of, one's good name; and it seems too that the declaratory sentence of the crime is to be referred to the moment when the crime was committed, so that from that time, elections, collations, or acquisitions of benefices, and even all legitimate acts are invalid. Exception is made for occult infamy and for acts of public office and jurisdiction, which are sustained by title of public office in favor of the common good. Although one who has incurred infamy of law ferendae sententiae should not be elected, the election is not ipso jure null, and if confirmed before a declaration has been pronounced, the confirmation is lawful—though the delinquent can afterwards be punished according to the gravity of the crime, even with privation of the dignity. If the infamy is latae sententiae, the election is ipso jure null, but until juridically pronounced it is tolerated by the Church, and the confirmation prevails under title of public

---

[1] Conc. Trid. sess. 24, c. 12.
[2] Matt. xxiii-23.
[3] Suarez, ib. 4, sect. 1, n. 11; Sylvester v. infamia n. 7.

office, but by a subsequent declaration of the crime, the election, confirmation, and all acts not pertaining to public office become void. Infamy has no effect in the elections of the Order of Friars Preachers until a juridical sentence has been given.[1]

XIII. Privation of passive voice, juridically pronounced, is also an impediment to canonical promotions. A superior cannot deprive any one of passive voice from extrajudicial knowledge, but he may refuse to confirm one whom he thinks unfit for an office. It is only per accidens that electors are bound in conscience not to elect a person not judicially deprived of voice, for example, if he is impenitent and manifestly unqualified, or by reason of scandal, or to avoid contentions and injury to the common good. The person himself, even though ipso jure but not juridically deprived of voice, is not bound in conscience to refuse his consent to an election, for no law obliges one to the execution of grave penalties before he has been sentenced to them. Exception is made for cases in which charity would bind him to refuse his consent.[2]

XIV. A person, whose election was at any time vetoed owing to a personal impediment, is ineligible. If the election was cassed by reason of a defect either in the form or in the electors, the candidate may be reelected in the same church or in another. One rejected from election by reason of a personal impediment contracts infamy of fact. It does not follow, however, that if a person be rejected from one election, he thereby remains universally rejected from all future elections, for rejection may arise from any one of three reasons: from a convicted crime, from a presumed crime, or from defect of age, infirmity and the like. The first two impediments are wiped out by penance, the third by cessation of the impediment.[3] In the Order of Friars Preachers where superiors are not accustomed to state their reasons for cassing an election, the electors should not elect one previously rejected in some other election, unless they are sure that the rejection was occasioned by a defect in the form.

XV. If there are persons in a diocese or province qualified for an office, outsiders should not be elected. But the election of an outsider is valid unless a special law or custom render it otherwise, and should be confirmed if there be no other impediment.[4] General chapters can abrogate contrary customs not approved by

[1] Passerini n. 595.
[2] ib. n. 606.
[3] cap. Super eo 12 de elect.
[4] Cap. Cum inter 21.

apostolic authority.[1] In the Order of Friars Preachers, brothers of one convent may be elected prior of another, and brothers of one province may be elected prior or provincial in another province, provided they meet the other required conditions.[2]

Since the free disposition of benefices belongs to the pope, he may confer them on whom he will; other superiors must follow special laws and customs. But should there be no one in a diocese or province qualified for an office, the superior—notwithstanding special laws and customs to the contrary—should select an outsider, for the necessity of choosing the one best fitted for an office is based on natural and divine law, against which positive law or custom has no force.[3]

XVI. The candidate must not be already assigned to another office or benefice. We shall consider this condition later when speaking of postulation.

XVII. No person can lawfully or validly elect himself.[4] Neither can any one present himself to a benefice. A father may present his son and where there are several patrons, one may present another. If a bishop confer a benefice on a patron, he may accept it; he may even request the bishop to confer it, for he does not thereby present himself.

There is only one instance in which a candidate may elect himself, namely by consenting to the election of himself by others, thus increasing the number of votes so as to constitute a majority.[5] But this does not hold where the form of the chapter "Quia propter," or secret ballot must be observed, according to which a candidate may not know he has been choosen by the others before the publication of the scrutiny, and a vote given outside the scrutiny is invalid. Hence this exception holds only where election is by public vote, or where an accessus is admitted after the publication of the scrutiny.

In addition to the above conditions for eligibility, the Constitutions of the Friars Preachers further require: 1° that a person does not dwell outside the Order, even with the permission of superiors, as explained above in the chapter on active voice. Such a person cannot be elected until one continuous year after his return,[6] and if he remained outside without the permission of

[1] Passerini ib. n. 656.

[2] Avignon, 1442.

[3] Passerini ib. n. 660.

[4] cap. In scripturis 8, q. 1.

[5] Cap. Cum in jure 33, de elect.

[6] Rome, 1580.

superiors, he remains ineligible for ten years, except by written permission of the master general. Apostates cannot be elected to any office before twenty years from their return; 2° that he has not refused the office of novice-master, and that he be not novice-master at the time of his election, unless with permission of the provincial; 3° that he does not immediately succeed a brother-german; 4° that he be not visitor general or his companion, or vicar of the election sent from another convent in case of necessity; 5° that he has never been prior in the convent of election, or that six years have elapsed since that time; 6° that in an episcopal city and in a House of Studies he be a lector in theology. In the first case the provincial may grant a dispensation, in the second the general.

CHAPTER VI

The Act of Election

When an election becomes necessary, the president must summon the electoral body to some specified place, and for a certain day within the legal time-limit. The place does not enter into the substance of election, still it should be held in a suitable place. Episcopal elections must take place within the church or its limits, unless there be a sufficient reason for holding it elsewhere.[1] Papal elections held outside the conclave are invalid.[2] If the majority of electors, for reasons of personal convenience, select a place outside the church limits, the minority are not bound to accede, but may appeal. If on the contrary, the customary place is not safe, the minority, nay even one, may compel the majority to choose a safe place.[3] It belongs to the president to determine just what place within the limits the election will be held. Should the electors conduct an election in an unsuitable place, as in the home of a secular power, they sin mortally, or at least venially, according to the degree of its unfitness. The election itself is not ipso facto null, but it should be annulled, for what is contrary to law should not obtain force. Clandestine elections—those not held publicly and collegiately,—are reprobated by law, and are null and void.[4] They are not ipse jure null, but reprobated in this sense, that the clandestinity must be remedied before they can be confirmed. Previous to an election in the Order of Friars Preachers, the superior asks if the place and time appointed by him be agreeable to all, and the majority disapproving, the election does not proceed.

The time appointed for holding an election presupposes the vacancy of the office or benefice in consequence of death, transfer, resignation or deposition. A prelate cannot be deposed unless by the declaration of a superior, and if he appeals, the sentence must be suspended. Consent to transferral or resignation does not render an office vacant until it has been accepted by a superior. Citation of vocals made before the prelacy is vacant

---

[1] cap. Quod sicut 28. de elect.

[2] Greg. XV. "Aeterni Patris."

[3] cap. Bonae 23, n. 1.

[4] cap. Quia propter.

is null, and does not revive on the death or removal of a prelate. Elections cannot be held prior to the funeral obsequies of a deceased prelate, unless there be a reasonable cause, but whether an election thus held should be annulled is greatly disputed. Regulars by privilege are not held to this last solemnity.[1]

The time fixed by law for the election does not begin from the vacancy of the office, but from the time of its becoming known—the determination of which time, rests with the judgment of the superior. Superiors are not held to notify the electors juridically of a prelate's death, for they are supposed to learn of it by ordinary means, but if the office becomes vacant in any other way, juridical notification must be given.[2]

The time-limit differs for different churches and orders, hence each should observe its own statutes and customs. Common law allows three months for the election of a bishop,[3] and if not held within this time it devolves on the superior. Other benefices should be provided for within six months. If the chapter does not elect a bishop within three months, or if a bishop does not provide for vacant benefices within six months provision in both these cases devolves to the metropolitan.

Religious orders, for the most part, follow their own particular statutes in this regard. In the Order of Friars Preachers elections of conventual priors must take place within one month from the knowledge of the vacancy, otherwise they devolve to the provincial who must appoint a prior within three months. A period of one year is given for a provincial election. If the electors do not elect or postulate a provincial within this time, and on the very day for which the electors are cited, the election ipso facto devolves to the master general. If a provincial dies or is removed in the first year of his office, and before Septuagesima, the vicar of the province must summon the vocals within the coming Septuagesima, to a chapter to be held after Easter; if he dies or is removed after Septuagesima, this convocation must be made in the following Septuagesima. If he should die or be removed in the last year of office, the vicar completes the term.[4] In many provinces the day assigned for the election of a new provincial is the Saturday before the second Sunday after the Octave of Easter.[5] The election of a master general should

[1] Lezana—Praedicatorum 7, n. 17.
[2] Passerini, c. 13, n. 7.
[3] cap. Ne pro defectu.
[4] Rome, 1841.
[5] Const. n. 838.

be held on the vigil of Pentecost. If a general dies or is removed after Pentecost, but before or on the feast of Saint Michael, a new general must be elected the following Pentecost; but if he dies after the feast of Saint Michael but before Pentecost, the election will not take place until the Pentecost of the following year—unless other dispositions are made by the authority of the Holy See, or unless the general dies in the twelfth year of office.[1] The general himself before completing his term gives due notification to the vocals of an approaching election, except in case of his death, when the vicar of the order issues the citation.[2] The election of a general devolves to the Holy See if not held on the day fixed by law, unless grave necessity renders this impossible. Definitors are elected any time during the provincial chapter. A socius of a prior to a provincial chapter may be elected any time between Septuagesima and the approach of the chapter on a day assigned by the sub-prior.

Elections may be held on feast days, for they are extrajudicial acts. For a reasonable cause they may be celebrated at night, there being no law to the contrary. Special law and customs requiring elections to be held during the day must be respected.

On the appointed day the superior or president opens the electoral assembly. Previous to the election of a bishop prayers and supplications are offered.[3] These exercises usually consist of a Mass of the Holy Ghost, reception of Holy Communion by all the electors and an invocation of the Holy Ghost by the antiphon "Veni Sancte Spiritus" or by the hymn "Veni Creator." In the Order of Friars Preachers a Mass of the Holy Ghost is offered before the elections of generals and provincials, and in every election an invocation to the Holy Ghost is made by the antiphon "Veni Sancte Spiritus" and the hymn "Veni Creator." A Mass of the Holy Ghost also usually precedes the election of a conventual prior. If an election should be cassed or if a person elected should refuse his consent, the Mass of the Holy Ghost is not repeated before the subsequent scrutiny.

Mass of the Holy Ghost and reception of Holy Communion do not belong to the substance of election—for there is no law nullifying elections not preceded by these exercises—unless special statutes prescribe them under pain of nullity. Nevertheless, to omit them is a grave or slight sin in proportion to the

[1] Ib. n. 753.

[2] Ib.

[3] Conc. Trid. sess. 24, c. 1 de ref.

scandal occasioned thereby. In the Order of Friars Preachers electors of provincials, conventual priors, or prioresses are obliged to communicate on the day of election under pain of privation of voice ipso facto incurred.[1] Elections not preceded by an invocation of the Holy Ghost and reception of Holy Communion by the electors are to be annulled if opposition is made.[2]

The spiritual exercises over, the assembly proceeds, if necessary, to verify the credentials of the electors. It is the office of the judge appointed by the statutes or customs of different colleges to decide whether the vocals are here and now qualified to vote. In admitting and excluding them the judge must proceed according to law and not from fact alone. No one can be deprived of his right to vote unless it is juridically evident that he does not possess the right. The judge cannot pass judgment on credentials coming from a higher authority, hence he cannot examine apostolic letters or pronounce sentence on their validity unless deputed by the pope to do so. Opposition, however, can be made to them until they are justified before the one commissioned to examine them,—the burden of proof resting with the opposing party.[3] The same is to be said proportionately of the letters of other superiors, which should be respectfully received. If they are given with condition of justification, the vocal must justify them before he can be admitted to vote. When, however, he possesses the right to vote by virtue of his letters, he is presumed to have justified them.[4] Hence, one in possession cannot be ejected unless his opponent furnishes clear proof that he has not justified his credentials. If the letters are given absolutely, the vocal is freed from the burden of proving them, and the chapter cannot impede their execution, unless their falsity is evident.

In the Order of Friars Preachers before the electors proceed to the election of definitors or to the celebration of a provincial chapter, certain ones are appointed by the provincial or vicar with the provincial council to examine the testimonial letters of those coming to the chapter, but no power is given them to exclude any one from active voice.[5] These examiners are called judges of voice (judices vocem). Their authority extends only to the examination of the letters which socii and priors are required by law to bring to the chapter. The power of excluding those not approved by these judges, rests with the president of the elec-

[1] Samuel, Tract 1, disp. 2, n. 6.
[2] Donatus III, Tract 1, q. 18, n. 11.
[3] Passerini, c. 14, n. 60.
[4] Rota, decis. 154, n. 2. coram Eminentissimo Ottobono.
[5] Rome, 1650.

tion, who has full jurisdiction in this regard.[1] Neither have the judges absolute authority in respect to the testimonial letters, for the judgment of the more serious difficulties belongs to the president and provincial council.[2] They can deprive no one of voice on account of any fault, nor declare any one deprived except priors and socii for one of the three following reasons: because they did not bring the prescribed testimonial letters; because the letters were false; or because they were not sufficient to meet the requirements of the law.[3] In provincial chapters they can examine the title of the socius, and in general chapters those of the definitors and electors.[4] All other matters concerning the vocals pertain to the provincial and provincial council. The provincial or vicar can also examine the testimonial letters of the priors and socii. Once the electoral body has been assembled, messengers may not be dispatched to inquire whether the vocals lawfully possess voice, but the election must proceed, and the doubts—if there be any—are sent to the confirming prelate.[5]

Then follows a discussion of the matters pertaining to the election. This discussion is not essential to the election, except where special statutes so prescribe. The voice of the electors, if not already attended to, is now legalized. Then deliberations are held concerning the time and place of election—in the Order of Friars Preachers the president asks the vocals if the time and place appointed are agreeable to them. Next there takes place a frank and free discussion of the merits of the candidates. The latter need not have previously made known their candidacy, though they may do so.[6] The electors are free to propose and sustain the candidates of their choice. If any one wishes to protest against the election, the active voice of the vocals or the passive voice of the candidates, his protestation or opposition is now considered, as well as the replies to the same. The president also makes a protestation that he does not intend to admit unqualified, or to exclude qualified vocals from the election. This having taken place, the president ad cautelam, then gives general absolution from all censures.

These preliminaries over, three members of the assembly worthy of trust are selected to examine secretly and separately

[1] Passerini, Ib., n. 67.
[2] Sylvester—Judex, n. 1.
[3] Passerini, Ib., n. 73.
[4] Ib., n. 70.
[5] Fontana, De Elect. n. 3.
[6] Boudinhon, Cath. Ency.

the votes of all. These are called scrutineers, because they scrutinize the votes of the others. They are chosen by the majority of the vocals, but custom can prescribe otherwise. In the Order of Friars Preachers the Constitutions provide for their institution; in the election of a prior or socius they are the sub-prior and vicar or the two oldest vocals.[1] The same holds for the election of a provincial elector. In the election of definitors of a general or provincial chapter they are the provincial or vicar of the province together with the prior and sub-prior of the convent in which the election is held, or at least two of these three; if the prior and sub-prior cannot be present, then the two oldest electors act as scrutineers. In the election of a provincial these officials are the three oldest priors, in that of a general the three oldest provincials.

The scrutineers are not to be elected according to the form of the chapter "Quia propter," but by public suffrage when they are not appointed by the superiors. In the Order of Friars Preachers, if the sub-prior has no voice or if one of those appointed, even though present, is impeded, a fourth is elected by public vote,[2] except in the province of Poland, where he is elected secretly by decree of the general made at the request of the provincial. If the one impeded is not present, then the three oldest present are chosen, this is also true when one of the oldest does not wish to act. Where there are but three vocals, two scrutineers suffice; where there are but two, one suffices; where there is but one, none are required. In all other cases there must be three. Although the form of election requires that there be no more than three, still the election of a fourth, fifth, or sixth though useless, does not vitiate an election. A general chapter may prescribed, unless expressly forbidden, that a fourth be elected, for the Lateran Council[3] forbade that a fourth be chosen by the electors but not by superiors having the right to make laws.

The Council of Trent decreed that in the election of all "superiors, temporal abbots and other officials, generals, abbesses, prioresses and other superioresses," all should be elected by secret vote and the names of the electors never published, and that all elections otherwise conducted are invalid.[4] This decree does not include the electors of bishops and perpetual abbots.

[1] Const. n. 553.
[2] Rome, 1629.
[3] cap. Quia propter.
[4] sess. 25 de Regul. c. VI.

The practice now is that generals, provincials and local prelates are elected according to the Tridentine form, but other officials are sometimes elected by public suffrage. In the Order of Friars Preachers, generals, provincials, priors, definitors of general and provincial chapters, the socius of a prior to a provincial chapter and electors of provincials and generals are elected by secret ballot, other elections are either by public or secret vote—not however, by ballot, but with black and white beans.

A much disputed question here arises whether the Tridentine decree admits of auricular scrutiny or whether the scrutiny be necessarily by ballot. Some hold that the decree absolutely forbids auricular scrutiny, and that elections not conducted by ballot are invalid.[1] They base their opinion on a statement made viva voce to Cardinal Cribello by Pius V (May 12, 1562), in which he declared that the mind of the Council prescribed secret vote by ballot.

But the majority of authors hold the contrary opinion,[2] which seems to be more probable. For it is generally admitted that the discipline of the Lateran Council was not abolished by that of the Council of Trent. But the former council merely called for the appointment of three trustworthy scrutineers, who should collect secretly and in quick succession the votes of all the electors.[3] The Sacred Congregation of the Council also considered an election secret when three or four receive the votes of the others.[4] The only extension the Council of Trent made to the discipline of the former council is that the votes given secretly in the scrutiny should never be published. But this decision is not in the least repugnant to auricular scrutiny, for it is one thing for the scrutineers to know the votes of the electors, which the council does not forbid, and quite another thing to publish them, which the council does forbid. To say that the votes are published when known to the scrutineers is contrary to the councils themselves, and also to the declarations of the Sacred Congregation of the Council. Furthermore, the cited declaration of Pius V is not sufficient for a contrary opinion, for even granted that it be authentic, all viva voce declarations were recalled by Gregory XV and Urban VIII. Another proof for our opinion is that the Council of Trent declared that elections of abbesses made by auricular vote to a bishop or superior listening

[1] Miranda II, q. 23, a. 15; Castell., Ib., c. 4. n. 62; Donatus III, tract. 1, q. 6. n. 7.

[2] Sigismund, Suarez, Garzias, Barbosa, Lavorius, Sc. Conc.

[3] cap. Quia propter.

[4] Suarez IV, t. 8, l. 2. n, 10.

at a small window were valid.[1] And since the Tridentine decree includes the election of abbesses, we cannot say that other elections by auricular vote are invalid.

The publication of votes in the election itself destroys its secrecy and makes it null and void. This publication would happen: 1°—if the election was conducted without scrutineers; 2°—if the vocals should make their choice known to the scrutineers in a voice so loud as to be heard by the other capitulars; 3°—if the scrutineers were not members of the chapter; 4°—if when announcing the result they should make known the names of the electors; 5°—if the electors' names were made known in the letters of confirmation—for election continues until it has been confirmed. The election is also invalid if the vote of but one elector is made public in the election, even with the permission of the major part. If, however, the majority object to this publicity, the election is valid, but the vote publicly given is invalid. But if the one thus publicly voting repent of his misdeed, he may be permitted to take part in the same election, provided he does not vote for the same candidate.[2] Such elections are invalid even though the vocal himself or the chapter be unaware of the defect.

Elections by ballot are invalid if any mark on a ballot or any circumstance connected with it, will acquaint one or more of the scrutineers with the name of the voter. In auricular elections scrutineers may know the names of electors, but in elections by ballot this knowledge is forbidden. The election is not invalid when one or more cast marked ballots unknown to and without the consent of the chapter. But if the chapter, aware of the fact, withhold its consent, the election is neither void nor voidable, though the unlawful votes must not be computed with the others. For where the majority elects rightly, and the minority sins—even in the form, this is not prejudicial to the election, unless especially decreed—as in the case where simony enters into an election.[3]

In the Order of Friars Preachers elections must be by secret ballots received in a receptacle by the scrutineers, who count, read, and burn them.[4] Ballots having any distinguishing mark are forbidden under pain of privation of active and passive voice, but if these votes are in the minority and were cast contrary to

---

[1] Ib. c. 7.

[2] Passerini, Ib., c. 17, n. 14.

[3] Ib. n. 21.

[4] Bologna, 1564.

the knowledge and wishes of the majority, the elections are neither void nor voidable, but the votes must be rejected.[1]

It is directly opposed to the substance of election for one elector to cast a vote, either orally or in writing, for another, unless it is manifest he was deputed to do so as procurator. Election, therefore, in its substance ought to proceed by votes secretly given by the vocals and secretly received by the scrutineers—and among religious, never published even after the election. Manifestation of the voters' names, however, made outside the election, provided it is not made by the scrutineers, is not forbidden either by the Lateran or Tridentine Councils. Absolutely speaking and making exception for particular statutes, it does not pertain to the substance of election to burn the ballots. In the Order of Friars Preachers they must be burned in the presence of the chapter before the result of the scrutiny has been announced, but even if burned after this announcement has been made, the election is valid. They are also burned in papal elections.

Some canonists question the validity of elections in which there are but two or three vocals. The common opinion is that such elections are valid, if not forbidden by particular statutes. For these elections are secret if the scrutineers receive the votes of each, or if the ballots are secretly cast; it is only accidental that, owing to the fewness of electors, their names are consequently manifested. In the Order of Friars Preachers no one from the electoral body present, or absent through his own fault, can be elected if there are less than five vocals, for to elect one of the chapter a majority of one and a half is required, which cannot be had when less than five are present.

Common law does not forbid voting by proxy, provided the mandate is not given for a definite person or persons, because in this case the election could not be secret, for it would always be certain that the procurator did not elect nor could not have elected one other than the person or persons named.[2] An absent vocal may, however, insinuate by word to the procurator the one for whom he wishes him to vote, and the procurator is bound in conscience to vote for the one thus named, but if he votes for another he acts validly. In this case the procurator could vote for two candidates, casting one vote for the candidate named by him whose procurator he is, and another for the candidate of his own choice.[3]

[1] Barcelona, 1574.

[2] Garzias V, c. 4, n. 199.

[3] Ib., n. 103.

Before the scrutineers begin the scrutiny they should take an oath that they will faithfully discharge their duties. But this oath is not essential, and in many instances is omitted. The place of scrutiny must be public and in sight of the whole chapter, but at such a distance from the electors that neither the electors talking to the scrutineers, nor the latter talking among themselves can be heard. In the Order of Friars Preachers an elector when casting his ballot may not put his hand into the urn, but the casting of the ballot must be plainly seen by the scrutineers.[1]

Recourse to lots in places not bound by the discipline of the chapter "Quia propter" does not render an election void, but rather voidable, and may be introduced by custom.[2] In other places elections so conducted are ipso jure invalid. Arbitrators may be elected through lots.[3]

It matters not by what words the formula is expressed, provided the elector expresses his consent de praesenti for a certain person. Three different formulas are given by authors: I elect N; I consent in N; I name N. All formulas implying indetermination or condition are worthless. Useless votes must be rejected, for example, a ballot naming the pope for the office of prior.

In auricular scrutiny the electors may make a new choice before the scrutiny has been committed to writing, and even when it has been committed to writing they may still recall their vote if the result has not been announced, provided that at least two of the scrutineers have a distinct recollection of their former choice. No retraction can be made once the result has been published.[4] In scrutiny by ballot only the one to cast his vote first may recall it, and that only when his vote alone is in the urn, for after a second vote has been cast revocation is forbidden. With the consent of the chapter all the votes may be burned at the instance of one vocal, and a new scrutiny taken. Furthermore, if prior to the announcement of the scrutiny the majority wish to have the ballots burned, this may be done and a new ballot taken. After the publication, no change is permitted, except when it is certain the election is null, in which case revocation is lawful provided it take place before the election is announced in the name of the college.[5]

---

[1] Const. n. 557.
[2] Passerini, Ib., c. 28, n. 6.
[3] Thesaurus II, v. elect. c. 2.
[4] Sigismund, Ib. dub. 29, n. 4; Sylvius, Ib. II, n. 7.
[5] cap. Cum terra 14, de elect. n. 4.

Every elector physically or morally present must vote, for the omission of one such vote is contrary to the substance of election.[1] A fourth scrutineer should not be appointed to receive the votes of the other three, but the latter must attend to the votes of one another. In the Order of Friars Preachers the scrutineers vote first, which prescription would be useful in all canonical elections.

Although the electors are in duty bound to vote for him whom they deem the most worthy among those qualified for the office in question, still they are not absolutely bound to take an oath to this effect. Clement VIII and Urban VIII prescribed an oath for religious electors, but the decree was not universally received. In the Order of Friars Preachers electors do not take an oath. When an absent religious elects by proxy, it is the procurator who takes the oath, but to do so he needs a special mandate. Outside of religious institutes either the absentee or the procurator having a special mandate takes the oath.

After the ballots have been cast they are counted, and their number compared with the number of voters. If they do not agree the ballots are burned and a new scrutiny taken. It is essential that the votes of the electors be committed to writing.[2] It suffices for one scrutineer to write the votes, but in order to avoid mistakes, it is better that all of them take a note of the count. Should there be a disagreement of count in scrutiny by ballot, the votes should be read a second time and the true number ascertained, but in auricular scrutiny, the written count of two obtains, but if all three disagree the scrutiny must be repeated. Written accounts of the scrutiny are not essential to all elections.[3]

The discipline of the chapter "Quia propter" must always be observed except in cases where its observance is impossible.[4] Hence, when there are less than four vocals the form prescribed cannot be observed,—for the scrutineers and the vocals not being distinct—the election cannot be known to the former without necessarily being made known to the latter. Where there is but one elector no scrutiny is required, for in one and the same act he may nominate, elect and publish the election, and it will suffice if in the presence of witnesses or letters before witnesses and notary, he says: In place of the college I elect N.[5] Where

[1] Passerini, Ib., n. 42.
[2] cap. Quia propter.
[3] Rota, decis. 289, n. 30, par. 6.
[4] Innoc. Ib., n. 6; Donatus, tract. 1, q. 17, n. 7.
[5] Panormitanus, Ib., c. 2.

a member of the electoral body must be chosen, and that body be reduced to one, there can be no election, for a vocal is forbidden to elect himself; but in this case he is considered elected by law, and the only thing required is the confirmation of the election thus made,[1] or that the confirming prelate appoint him to the office in question.[2] When an election devolves to a superior he should choose one having the qualities required by the college. Hence, when the candidate should be selected from the college, and the college be reduced to one, that one should be chosen. When ineligibles may be reinstated by a superior, then the one remaining vocal is not ipso jure elected, nor is the superior bound to select him, but may if he so desire, rehabilitate the former to passive voice and the qualified vocal may elect one of the number, or the superior could rehabilitate them to both active and passive voice, and then recourse must be had to the customary election.[3]

When the electoral assembly consists of but two members, these two are not held to the law of scrutiny, but may elect publicly without having recourse to scrutiny, which would be superfluous and useless. If a member of the college must be chosen, then one should renounce his vote and, if elected by the other, the election is valid unless prohibited by special statute.[4] In the latter case the election devolves to the superior who is bound to choose one of the two. When there are three electors they are not bound to observe the discipline of the chapter "Quia propter," except to elect by ballot when prescribed by special law, and not to publish the names of the electors outside of the college.[5]

We have said above that after all the votes had been cast they are counted, and this is true even when all are given for the same person, since it is absolutely essential that the number of votes tally with the number of electors. In former times, the candidate who had obtained the votes of the more numerous and sounder part (major et sanior pars) of the college, was declared elected. Although it was presumed that the more numerous part was the sounder part also, still contrary proof was admitted, and this appreciation, necessitating a comparison not only of the number of votes but also of the merits and zeal of the electors, led to endless discussions and dissensions. But the subsequent use

---

[1] Cuth. IV, de elect. n. 3.
[2] Sigismund, Ib., dub.23, n. 8.
[3] Passerini, Ib., n. 70.
[4] Sigismund, Ib., d. 23, n. 5.
[5] Passerini, Ib., n. 75.

of the secret and written ballot proved an efficient remedy to these difficulties by assuring the election to the candidate who obtains an absolute majority or two-thirds. When the electors are odd in number a gain of one vote constitutes a majority; if the number be even, a gain of two votes is required.[1] In the Order of Friars Preachers if the candidate is a member of the chapter and present therein, or if absent through his own fault, he must receive a gain of two votes to ensure the majority, but if legitimately impeded from being present, an absolute majority is sufficient, just as in the election of an outsider.[2] Vocals absent through their own fault, or those who renounce their vote, are not to be computed in the number of electors, but contemned vocals must be numbered in calculating the majority. Alternative, uncertain, useless and blank votes are not to be taken into account, for whoever casts such votes is considered to have forfeited his right for that ballot.[3] When two or more candidates receive the same number of votes, the choice of candidates is made by him to whom the chapter, law or custom commits this office. Sometimes the confirming prelate may choose the one he thinks best fitted for the office in question. Should no candidate obtain an absolute majority, another scrutiny is held, and so on until a decisive vote is reached. However, special statutes can prescribe, and in some cases have prescribed various remedies for useless balloting, for example, that after three rounds of fruitless balloting the election shall devolve upon the superior; or that in the third round the electors can vote only between the two most favored candidates; or that in the fourth round a relative majority shall suffice,—as in congregations of nuns under simple vows.[4]

When the final vote has been counted and committed to writing, the result should be officially announced to the electoral body by the presiding officer or by one deputed thereto.[5] This act is also essential. The time within which it should take place is left to the judgment of the superior, provided there be no definite time prescribed by special statute. The vocals are not obliged to remain in the chapter while the votes are being read. Outsiders may be present when the announcement is made. The first scrutineer or the one appointed by custom or statute, then

---

[1] Boudinhon, Ib.,

[2] Avila, 1895.

[3] Sigismund, Ib., d. 9, n. 11.

[4] Boudinhon, Ib.

[5] cap. Quia propter.

announces accurately how many votes were cast for each candidate, and this done, he then in a clear voice in his own and in the name of the chapter, formally elects the candidate who obtained the required majority of votes.

The decree of election is next drawn up, and dispatched to the confirming prelate. This decree is a written document containing a complete account of the electional proceedings. It is commonly held that it does not enter into the substance of election. Castellini says he knows of many instances when the process of elections in the Order of Friars Preachers was announced orally to the superior by one or more of the scrutineers.[1] Common law requires that "instructors" accompany the decree in order to explain its details, but the majority of authors hold that this applies only to elections which are to be confirmed by the Apostolic See. The decree is ordinarily, but not necessarily, signed by all the electors. In the Order of Friars Preachers the scrutineers in presence of the whole chapter sign and seal the document, which is then sent as soon as possible to the superior by a messenger. No vocal is permitted to convey the document, under pain of privation of active and passive voice, and of the punishment imposed on those journeying without permission.[2]

Before passing to the next chapter we must say a few words about those two exceptional modes of election, namely compromise and quasi-inspiration.

Compromise occurs when all the electors confide the election to one or several ecclesiastics, either members of the chapter or strangers, and ratify in advance the choice made by the arbitrator or arbitrators. This method was excluded from the elections of regulars by the Council of Trent.[3] It is not necessary that the chapter appoint the arbitrators but it may commission others to do so.[4] If each one is given absolute power of electing, they are presumed to have been elected in solidum.[5] The compromise is conditional or absolute according as the arbitrators are or are not restricted. For the latter the unanimous consent of the chapter is required, for the former that of the majority suffices.[6]

All the conditions for election in general must be complied with in election by compromise, for what is necessary to the

---

[1] c. 12, n. 25-30.
[2] Valencia, 1647.
[3] sess. 25, de Regul. c. 6.
[4] Miranda, II, q. 33, a.34.
[5] Jo. Cald. Conf. 6.
[6] Passerini, Ib., c. 22, n. 20.

genus is necessary to the species. Arbitrators cannot be elected except by those electors collegiately united, who should, and would and can conveniently be present. In limited compromise they must be elected by secret vote.

The arbitrators cannot exceed the power granted them. This power may be revoked by the majority of the chapter re adhuc integra. When the arbitrators elect by scrutiny, their faculty may be revoked as often as the scrutiny is repeated, provided the faculty was not bestowed as a favor or honor, for in this case it is presumed to have been an irrevocable gift.[1] Tacit revocation is not sufficient, but if the chapter should elect re adhuc integra the election would prevail.

An arbitrator cannot elect himself, if he wishes to be a candidate he must renounce his office.[2] If the mandate permits one of the arbitrators to be elected, then half the number of votes together with his consent will ensure his election.[3] In election by secret scrutiny, not according to the chapter "Quia propter," no one can nominate himself in the scrutiny, but after the votes have been announced he may add his own to that already given to him, by recalling it from another, provided that his vote did not constitute a majority for the other.[4] Where the form "Quia propter" obtains, the consent of a candidate is never permitted to increase the number of votes cast for him. If the mandate forbids the election of an arbitrator, such an election would be null; if it contains no clause on this point he may be elected, provided the mandate does not call for an unanimous vote.

Should the arbitrators, even in good faith, elect an unworthy candidate, the power of electing returns to the chapter, if the lawfully prescribed time for the election has not already expired.[5] The same is true when the candidate refuses his consent. But if the aforesaid time expires and they have elected either an unworthy candidate or no candidate, the election devolves upon the superior.

When the arbitrators elect an unworthy candidate, they and not the electors are punished with suspension for three full years from all benefices possessed in the church in which the election took place. This punishment applies only in the elections of bishops and their superiors and not when an arbitrator is a bishop.

[1] Ib., n. 30.
[2] Sylvius, Ib., II, q. 16, n. 19.
[3] cap. In jure 33, de elect.
[4] Sylvester, electio 2, n. 2.
[5] Ib., n. 26.

When an arbitrator is likewise a confirming prelate he may by one and the same act elect and confirm a candidate.[1]

Inspiration, by which a person may be elected to an ecclesiastical office, is twofold. The one is called true inspiration by which a person is chosen by God through revelation properly so called, as in the case of Saint Matthias. The other is quasi or common inspiration, and is supposed to exist when, with no special preceding discussion on a certain person, the electors assembled in the electoral chamber unanimously and at the same time, with no contradiction or hesitation, immediately proclaim a person elected. For such unanimous consent is presumed to have come from the Holy Ghost—the Author of unity and concord. The customary general preceding discussion is not contrary to election by quasi-inspiration.[2]

If an elector is absent by reason of his having been contemned there can be no election by quasi-inspiration, even if after the election he should give his consent, for such consent is presumed to have been prompted by the influence of the others and not by the Holy Ghost. Neither can there be election by quasi-inspiration if one should recall his vote before the publication of the scrutiny, because the consent would be no longer unanimous.[3] A capitular may be elected by quasi-inspiration, if he consents to the election thus made, and this even if he had voted for another, because the vote of the elect is not computed, and hence does not destroy the required unanimity.[4]

Confirmation is not required when it is evident that the election was inspired by God, as in the case of Saints Ambrose and Nicholas. It pertains to the superior to decide this point, and the elect cannot assume office without his knowledge and permission. But the practice of today, as we stated on an earlier page, is that the Church will not ratify this method of election, knowing well that if the electors were prompted by the Holy Ghost, they will not hesitate to confirm their choice by secret vote,—the Holy Ghost still moving and inspiring.

[1] Passerini, Ib., c. 22, n. 52.

[2] Sylvester, n. 28.

[3] Hostiensis, de elect. "Qualiter facienda."

[4] Tabien., v. electio 3.

CHAPTER VII

Postulation

In ancient law there was but very little difference between the election and postulation of ecclesiastical prelates, for these words were used promiscuously.[1] Today they differ greatly, for they imply essentially distinct modes of providing for widowed churches. By election a candidate acquires a certain right, and his confirmation is an act of justice; by postulation he acquires no right, and his confirmation is a matter of favor. Election once concluded cannot be recalled, postulation, on the contrary, is always subject to recall until it has been presented to the superior. A candidate elect is worthy and eligible, a postulate is worthy but not eligible because he has an impediment. If some of the vocals elect, and others postulate a candidate, in order that the postulation prevail a majority of two-thirds is necessarily required. Hence postulation is defined as a petition of the chapter presented to a competent ecclesiastical superior that he promote to a vacant ecclesiastical office a person who is debarred from election, not on account of a personal defect, but be reason of some canonical impediment, which does not render him absolutely ineligible.[2] Since, therefore, these two modes of ecclesiastical provision agree in this, that both pertain to the chapter, yet differ essentially in the aforesaid points, it now remains—having exposed the method of election—to speak briefly of the other method which is postulation.

Postulation is either solemn or simple. The former is that defined in the preceding paragraph, and admitted by the superior has the force of a confirmed election. The postulate, therefore, after confirmation acquires the same right as though he had been elected and confirmed. The latter is merely a request made to a superior to obtain his consent for the promotion of a candidate subject to his jurisdiction, e. g., a religious.

Solemn postulation—differently from simple—ought to be made by the electors collegiately assembled, observing the canonical forms and statutes, and within the lawfully prescribed time for election. It is safer, though not necessary, to observe

---

[1] cap. Litteras dist. 63.

[2] D. Antoninus, 111., tit. 19, c. 3.

the form of scrutiny, except in religious orders, where it must be secret ballot. An absolute majority of votes constitutes a valid postulation.[1] Though it rarely or never occurs without a previous election, still it does not depend upon election. By special privilege—though contrary to common law—one candidate can be elected and another postulated at the same time.

The general rule in regard to active voice is that they who are qualified to elect, can also postulate, for postulation is accessory to election and necessarily connected with it. The postulation must be presented to the candidate within the prescribed time-limit, and the latter must give or refuse his consent within one month, otherwise he is presumed to have dissented. He can only give conditional consent, and although he can withhold it from the chapter, he cannot do so against the wishes of the Supreme Pontiff.

In regard to passive voice the general principle is that whoever is qualified for election cannot be postulated. All those are eligible for postulation who have an impediment from which the Holy See can and will dispense. If the impediment be doubtful, one can be elected and postulated, and this done the candidate then chooses the method by which he wishes to be promoted to the vacant office. Among those unqualified for postulation are infants, insane, and women, the offspring of an incestuous union, those less than twenty-seven years of age (if it be a question of episcopal postulation) and bishops who entered the religious state on account of having committed some crime. The Holy See usually grants dispensations from all other canonical impediments, hence those so unqualified may be postulated. Those qualified for simple postulation are cardinals, priests and deacons, regulars, prelates inferior to bishops and subject to them. Those who knowingly postulate an unworthy candidate lose, ipso facto, the right of postulating and electing for that election.

Postulation should be made to the superior in whose power it is to dispense from the impediment. A superior is bound to admit postulation made by the majority of vocals, if necessity of the church and the common good require it, and should he refuse, a higher authority may compel him to do so.[2] Before its admission the postulate cannot administer the office for which he was postulated, and should he do so the postulation is thereby ipso jure null and void.

[1] Hostiensis, de post. n. 10.

[2] Passerini, Ib. c. 24, n. 48.

The same elector cannot at the same time elect and postulate different persons.[1] If one candidate is elected by one-third of the electors, and another postulated by two-thirds, the postulation prevails, and the election must be cassed; if the postulate receives but one less than two-thirds, the election must be confirmed.[2] But if the candidate postulated by two-thirds majority be unworthy, then both the postulation and election are void, except when the majority of those two-thirds knowingly postulated said candidate, in this case the election must be confirmed. Passerini says the discipline of the chapter "Scriptum" is particular legislation, and that whenever a person is elected by the majority of vocals, the election should be confirmed, but if the one postulated receive the majority the superior may, if he sees fit, reject the postulation, unless necessity or the common good require him to admit it.

Besides this postulation ex jure, there is also postulation ex privilegio, which is that conceded to the Order of Friars Preachers by Alexander IV, March 16, 1257, and by virtue of which three concessions are given over and above those granted by common law: 1° the vocals may elect one and postulate another at one and the same time; 2° they may postulate several persons; 3° they may postulate an eligible candidate. The superior may admit any one of those postulated. But this postulation holds only where there is also an election, for the decree expressly states that it is to be admitted, if for any reason the election is not confirmed. This privilege does not abolish that which common law concedes, namely, that if the vocals do not wish to elect they may have recourse to postulation, for a privilege does not take away what the common law denies.[3] But in case they do not wish to elect, they must observe the laws of the sacred canons concerning postulation—if they resort to postulation.

This privilege comprehends only the elections of conventual priors and provincials. The postulation must be by secret ballot, and on the same ballot the vocal first writes the name of the person he wishes to elect by the words: I elect N. (Eligo N.), and then writes the name of the postulate after the words: I postulate N. (Postulo N.). Then there should be observed all those acts prescribed to be observed in the scrutiny of election. In the decree of election the scrutineer should write: Ego N. eligo N. et postulo N. A majority of votes suffices for postulation, ex-

[1] De post. in VI.
[2] cap. Scriptum 40, de elect.
[3] Passerini, Ib. n. 65.

cept when the postulate is a member of the chapter, when a gain of two or one and a half votes is required (Bologna, 1564) if he be present or not legitimately absent.

As said above, postulation can be admitted only when the election for some reason is not confirmed. The election is therefore to be examined first, for postulation is never admitted by virtue of an inequality of suffrage alone, but election should always be preferred unless there be a good reason to the contrary. If it happen that the election is not confirmed, the superior is not bound to admit postulation, for the privilege grants the faculty but does not impose the necessity of admitting postulation. And since postulation is based on favour and not on justice, the person postulated acquires no right to the prelacy, though the practise of the order is that the superior usually admits one of the postulates when he cannot reasonably confirm the election.

If an election is null from defect of form, postulation is likewise invalid, for the form of both is one and the same. Postulation presupposes an election canonical in appearance, but not necessarily an absolutely valid election. Custom—which is the best interpreter of laws—has always understood and still understands this privilege to be such, that where no one is canonically and lawfully elected, postulations ex privilegio are null and void.[1]

[1] Passerini, Ib. n. 74.

CHAPTER VIII

Defects in Election

The essence of election not only requires lawful qualification of active and passive voice and observance of canonical form, but also that it be absolutely free; in other words, the freedom of the electors must not be impaired by unjust laws, fraud, threats, or excessive fear. In order, therefore, to give a complete notion of canonical election, we must show how these vices are opposed to it and render it either void or voidable.

I. In regard to the persons eligible, election cannot be restricted to one specified candidate by any law, statute, or precept, for such an ordination is unjust and the electors are not held to obey it, and should they elect another worthy candidate, he must be confirmed. The nature of election requires a free choice of one in preference to another.[1] The common opinion of canonists is that the electors should have a choice of at least three, but this—though reasonable—is not absolutely essential. Many decrees of the Sacred Congregations state that elections cannot be restricted to less than four or five. All admit, however, that if a restriction is made with the unanimous consent of the electors, it is not contrary to liberty. So also if there should be but two candidates fully qualified, the electoral choice may be restricted to these two, for such objective restrictions come from divine law, which prohibits the election of an unworthy candidate. Some canonists even say that an election could be restricted to one for the same reason.[2] This has happened in the Order of Friars Preachers, where at one time there was but one brother qualified for the provincialate of Calabria, the general notified the electors that if they did not elect this brother, he would appoint an outsider. But such restrictions give rise to many difficulties, and should be made with the greatest prudence; and if another than the one designated should be elected, he must be confirmed, unless his unfitness be clearly proved.[3]

Restricted elections are not ipso jure null, for the electors can disregard the restriction and elect another. Even if through

---

[1] S. Th. Ia 2ae, qu. 13, art. 12.

[2] Donatus, tract. I, q. 10, n. 13.

[3] Passerini, Ib., c. 2, n. 17.

fear the vocals unwillingly elected a specified candidate, the election is valid—since fear does not destroy liberty—and can be annulled only at the instance of the electors. If they voted freely, the election is neither void nor voidable. Neither can elections be restricted to a certain class in such a way that the vocals could not elect one of another if they so wished. General chapters with the consent of the subjects or by apostolic authority can establish alternatives, in virtue of which a candidate must be chosen from one nation for this election, and from another for the next. Elections contrary to these alternatives are not ipso jure null—unless expressly so ordained—but voidable at the petition of the vocals.[1] The Roman Pontiff can restrict an election to one and under pain of nullity, for the right of election belongs to the Holy See.

In the Order of Friars Preachers provincials in case of necessity can restrict the electors to not less than three candidates, but not to the exclusion of others; for should they elect another, the provincial must confirm him, if he has the necessary qualifications.[2] Pius V decreed that if a general or provincial of the Order of Friars Minor restrict the electors to three or four candidates, he shall be deprived of office.[3] Generals in reforming provinces or congregations may, by special privilege, restrict the vocals to three or four candidates under pain of cassation, but this privilege is not conceded to the office, and must be obtained by each newly elected general if need arises.

II. In respect to the electors freedom of election is impaired when they are deprived of voice, their number increased or diminished.

No superior, the pope excepted, can deprive a lawful capitular of active voice, unless he proceeds according to the prescriptions of common law. The pope for a just cause can licitly and validly recall this concession, and even without a just cause, his revocation would be valid. In the Order of Friars Preachers no vocal can be lawfully deprived of voice within a month previous to any election, except for reasons given in the chapter on grave faults. A provincial's office expiring during the vacancy of the generalship, or after the beginning of a year fixed for a general chapter for which he is a definitor, continues until the general is elected, or the chapter has been held.[4]

---

[1] Ib., n. 60.
[2] Bologna, 1564.
[3] Miranda II, q. 23, a. 21.
[4] Castell., c. 5, n. 781.

Superiors cannot increase the number of electors by sending an outsider to an election, unless they have power to give approbation for active voice to persons not possessing it. In the Order of Friars Preachers this may be done in two cases, as we have stated above when treating of the conditions for active voice.[1] When, therefore, the number of electors is fixed by common law, no one inferior to the Pope may increase or lessen it; when it is not determined, it may be increased or lessened by those who have this right from common law. We have already seen that superiors of the Order of Friars Preachers cannot validly assign brothers with active voice to a convent from two months before the prior's term of office expires until the election and confirmation of a new prior.[2] Moreover, if a brother has been assigned to a convent two months previous to an election, this assignation must be made known to the convent. Superiors are forbidden to make simulated or fictitious assignations. There are some exceptions to this discipline, but they too have already been sufficiently treated on an earlier page.[3]

Just as there can be no assignations to, so also there can be no removals from a convent of the Order of Friars Preachers within two months previous to an election, unless necessity of providing for an office in another convent or grave scandal requires a removal. And if a vocal is removed for any reason within this time he retains his voice in the convent a quo, even though no longer assigned there. If after the election and confirmation of a prior, brothers are assigned to or removed from a convent, and some time later the election and confirmation are cassed, the election of a new prior does not pertain to those who here and now have been assigned to the convent for two months, but to those who were assigned thereto for two months previous to the former vacancy, for a priorship is considered vacant from the expiration of one prior's term of office until the lawful and valid election and confirmation of another.[4]

If a superior remove a vocal within the prohibited time, the election is licit and valid, if he was not excluded or contemned by the electoral body. Neither is the election voidable at the instance of the said vocal, for he suffered no injury from the electors, but from the superior.[5] But if he were excluded and con-

---

[1] vide p. 42, lit. b.
[2] Passerini, Ib. n. 50.
[3] vide p. 42.
[4] Castell., Ib. c. 5, n. 73.
[5] Passerini, Ib. n. 106.

temned by both chapter and superior, the election is voidable at his indictment. In case the number was unjustly increased, if it is evident the election was not decided by this circumstance, it is neither void nor voidable, for "utile per inutile non vitiatur." In doubt, the vocals should be admitted under protest.[1]

III. Freedom of election is also impeded by violence and fear. The former absolutely destroys free will and renders an act wholly involuntary. The latter implies a dread of evil, but does not absolutely force the will, it causes a person to will something, which he would not have willed, if he did not apprehend evil. Vocals are affected by the former if they are violently ejected from the capitular assembly, or compelled to cast a ballot against their will; by the latter when through fear of grave injury they are moved to vote for a particular candidate—being forced to choose a lesser in order to avoid a greater evil.

Violence and fear may be just or unjust: just when a vocal is compelled by legitimate authority to observe the prescriptions of the sacred canons; unjust when the legitimate liberty of the vocal is destroyed. Violence properly so-called renders an election null and void, since it destroys freedom of choice. If fear is justly and reasonably incited by superiors, elections thus affected are neither void nor voidable—even when the electors are restricted to one candidate, for the elector is not thereby absolutely necessitated to one, since fear does not destroy liberty and his act remains voluntary.[2] The common and most probable opinion is that elections brought about through fear unjustly excited are not ipso jure void but voidable, unless there be a special law to the contrary.[3] Grave fear unjustly directed to extort the votes of the electors is sufficient to annul an election.

All who unjustly persecute ecclesiastical vocals, for not having elected the candidate they proposed, incur the penalty of excommunication.[4] This censure is also extended to postulation and in a wide sense to presentation.[5]

IV. Many pontifical constitutions have been promulgated against those who procure the votes of electors by evil subornations or bribes. Clement VIII decreed that all who directly or indirectly procured votes in this way either for themselves or for others should be deprived of voice perpetually. Accomplices and

[1] Lezana, Ib. n. 107.

[2] St. Th. Ia IIae, qu. 6, art. 6, ad 2m.

[3] Passerini, Ib. c. 4, n. 10.

[4] Lateran Council.

[5] Passerini, Ib. n. 44.

those knowing but not revealing such actions also incur the penalty.[1]

Consultations of vocals rightly ordered according to justice and charity is not only not prohibited but prescribed. If an elector is in doubt as to which is the fittest candidate he may extol the virtues and the merits of the one, and in so far as justice will permit modestly recount the defects of the others. These discussions are evil and are to be reprobated if they take place before the office is vacant. In the Order of Friars Preachers one public discussion is allowed on the day previous to the election, but the vocals may engage in private discussions at will.

Provincials of the same order who endeavor to induce directly or indirectly electors to vote for unworthy candidates are punished with privation of active and passive voice and perpetual inhability to all dignities and offices.[2] Passerini, contrary to many other authors, holds that these public discussions on the merits of candidates are not necessary, except when ordered by the Supreme Pontiff, and that general chapters can prescribe under pain of excommunication latae sententiae that they be omitted.[3]

V. It is forbidden to bestow offices on regulars at the request of persons—secular or ecclesiastical—outside an order, or to procure office through their influence, for the interference of outsiders tends to bring discord and dissension into a community. Parents do not come under the name of outsiders.[4] The censures incurred by superiors sinning in this respect vary according to different institutes. It is certain that all sin mortally. Superiors of the Friars Minor, Hermits of St. Augustine, Carmelites, and of other orders incur excommunication latae sententiae.[5] The constitutions and ordinations of the Order of Friars Preachers mention no penalty, but the chapter of Rome 1589 and Milan 1622 warned superiors that such actions would bring upon them the guilt of mortal sin.

Subjects are forbidden to procure offices through the influence of outsiders, to accept those thus procured, or to bestow gifts for the purpose of obtaining them. Unprofessed novices and nuns are not comprehended in the pontifical decrees. In some orders members are permitted to procure offices for those

---

[1] Ib. c. 5, n. 31.

[2] Toulouse, 1628.

[3] Passerini, Ib. 65-73.

[4] Portell., n. 18.

[5] Ib. n. 1.

in the same order; in the Order of Friars Preachers it is forbidden to procure them either for oneself or for others.[1] To determine accurately the discipline regarding subjects, the different papal constitutions published for different orders must be considered. Subjects of the Order of Friars Preachers incur excommunication latae sententiae, perpetual privation of suffrages and all offices, and many grevious penalties.[2]

VI. One of the worst vices that can creep into canonical elections is simony. Simony is a deliberate intention of buying or selling for a temporal price such things as are spiritual or annexed unto spirituals.[3] Speaking of simoniacal elections we include all modes of ecclesiastical provision. Furthermore, if the first act of an election is simoniacal, so also are all subsequent acts. Purchase and sale are strictly required to constitute simony, for any exchange of spiritual for temporal things is simoniacal, e. g. elect me bishop, and I shall confer a benefice upon you. The general rule is that to impose any burden on a spiritual office not annexed to it is simony. It is not simony to give a temporal as a price of a spiritual thing, provided it was not the determining motive.[4]

The first censure pronounced against simoniacs,—even occult—is excommunication latae sententiae simply reserved to the Apostolic See, and affects: 1° those persons and their accomplices who are guilty of simony in ecclesiastical benefices, provided that the terms of the agreement have been partly or completely fulfilled by both parties; 2° all persons of whatsoever dignity who procure a benefice for a certain person with the agreement that the latter will later either resign the benefice in favour of him through whom it was procured, or divide the revenues with him; 3° those who buy or sell admission into a religious order.[5]

A simoniac is also suspended, but since he is already excommunicated, this censure is of little moment. He may likewise accidently incur irregularity from the fact that he is branded with infamy. He does not incur it per se, since irregularity is incurred only in cases expressly declared by law, and nowhere can we find such a declaration.

---

[1] Rome, 1589.

[2] Fontana, v. favores.

[3] St. Th. 2a 2ae qu. 100, art. 1.

[4] Suarez, n. 13.

[5] Const. "Apostolicae Sedis."

Infamy of law ferendae sententiae is another penalty of simony, and this once incurred brings with it irregularity. All simoniacal promotions even among regulars are affected by this censure. Simoniacs not only incur these grave penalties, but are also deprived—ferendae sententiae—of all offices and benefices.[1]

All ecclesiastical provisions tainted with simony are ipso jure null and void.[2] We except papal elections from this statement: Julius II declared these elections invalid but this enactment was rescinded by Pius X.[3] Both parties are bound to restitution. The purchaser is also bound in conscience to restore all profits actually acquired,[4] as well as those which but for his fault the rightful possessor would have acquired. He may, however, retain the expenses attached to the acquisition of the profits—except those expended in improving the benefice, and the salary due to his ministry. A simoniacal office becomes ipso facto vacant, and can be conferred on another without awaiting a sentence of declaration, for it is sufficient if declaration is made and proof furnished even after a new collation; but the condemned may appeal from the sentence, and if he does, he must not in the meantime be deprived of his office, though in conscience he sins in retaining it.

Persons who in good faith receive a simoniacal benefice must resign it together with the profits, except those consumed while in good faith. If, however, an enemy fraudulently gives money for the promotion of a person, so that the election will be cassed and the candidate punished, or if on hearing that simony was to enter into the election, said person expressly objects thereto, he lawfully and validly acquires the benefice, and is not held to renounce it, unless he afterwards consented to the agreement by carrying out its stipulations.[5] But if such an election favored the candidate, and unconscious of it he made no resistance, the acquisition is null, and as soon as the beneficiary learns of it, he is bound to resign both benefice and profits—even those consumed, in so far as he had thereby become richer.[6] But if he held the benefice for three years in the same good faith in which he had received it, he is in nowise bound to resign it.[7]

[1] cap. Presbyter 3.

[2] Paul II. "Cum detestabile."

[3] Const. "Vacante Sede," Dec. 25, 1904.

[4] St. Th. 2a 2ae qu. 100, art. 6, ad 3m.

[5] St. Th. Ib.

[6] Ib.

[7] Rota in Calagur. Dec. 14, 1592.

VII. The interference of secular power is also detrimental to the natural liberty of ecclesiastical elections. A person consenting to his being elected through abuse of secular power is deprived of office and becomes ineligible to all dignities unless he obtain a dispensation. Electors celebrating such an election render it invalid, are suspended from offices and dignities for three years, and deprived of active voice.[1] In the latter case bishops are excepted, for they do not fall under a general law of suspension. This decree refers only to elections to prelacies strictly so-called, hence does not include canonries, benefices with care of souls, or other offices not dignities.[2]

Election by abuse of secular power takes place when a lay person or power takes an active part in an election, exercises any office therein, or when his consent is required for the election of a certain person. If a lay person inspires fear to such an extent that he actually forces the electors to elect a candidate of his choice, or one of a certain class, the election is null and void; but if through grave fear he compel them to admit him into the chapter, to give him some office, or to obtain his consent, the election is valid, and the vocals are neither suspended nor deprived of voice.[3]

It is not an abuse of secular power: 1° if a layman takes part in an election from privilege, which can be granted by the pope; 2° if from privilege or custom lawfully prescribed a prince wishes to be notified of the death of a prelate, that the election take place only with his permission, or that his consent be asked for elections already held; 3° if from custom, privilege, or conditions placed when founding a benefice, the consent of the patron is required for elections therein. If the patron is a layman, this privilege can be conceded by the pope, if an ecclesiastic, by the bishop. A custom cannot, however, be introduced, in virtue of which a layman may be permitted to vote in ecclesiastical elections.[4] A custom cannot be introduced whereby an election held contrary to the wishes or without the consent of a prince would be ipso jure void or voidable.

The Council of Sardinia ordained that those who elect or postulate by the voice of the people, are for that time deprived ipso facto of suffrage, and the election—ipso juro null—devolves

---

[1] cap. Quisquis 43.

[2] Barbosa, de jure eccles. I. n. 19.

[3] Bonacius, de censuris, disp. 3, q. 4, p. 5, n. 4.

[4] Azorius, 11, 1, 6, c. 4, q. 18.

to those who were not guilty. Paschal II declared all who receive a benefice at the hands of a layman excommunicated.[1]

VIII. Ecclesiastical elections can also be vitiated by the non observance of the form and solemnities required by positive and canon law. A slight omission in the form does not vitiate the act. But where it is altered to a considerable extent, either by acting contrary to or not in accordance with it, the act is null. If, for a just impediment, the form prescribed by positive law is omitted, the election is valid, for it is repugnant to reason that positive law should bind one to the impossible, since such is contrary to the justice of law.[2]

When an election has been invalidly conducted because of the non observance of the form, and the vocals learn of the defect before a sentence has been pronounced, they can emend their fault and again lawfully elect, because by reason of the first defect alone, they were not ipso jure deprived of voice.[3] Moreover, if the majority sin against the form and wish to repair their fault, they may do so even against the opposition, protestations of nullity and appeal of the minority, for the majority does not lose its right nor the minority acquire a new right, before a sentence has been given to this effect. But once the election has been perfected, the vocals cannot proceed to a new election until the first shall have been cassed.

There are many other points regarding the form and solemnities of canonical elections, but since they have been already exposed in detail in the chapter on the act of election, to recount them here would be a useless repetition.

---

[1] cap. Si quis clericus.

[2] St. Th. 1a 2ae., q. 95, art. 2.

[3] Sylvester, Electio I. n. 3.

CHAPTER IX

Subsequent Acts

I. A canonical election is ipso jure null and void if, previous to the election, the one nominated in the scrutiny consented to his election. For to consent to an election at any time before the choice has been declared in the name of the chapter by the one appointed, is contrary to the prescriptions of the chapter "Quia propter." Hence, the electors cannot in the name of the chapter publicly ask for the consent of the person elected until the election has been closed. A private interrogation prior to the election is at times useful and laudable, but it must not be made in the name of the chapter.

If the election meets with no opposition on the part of those interested therein, common law prescribes that the presiding official notify the person elected that choice has been made of his person, and ask his consent. Regarding this notification special statutes and customs should be observed. In the Order of Friars Preachers no notification is made, even though the one chosen be present, nor is his consent required, but the document of election is sent to the superior, who—since the will of the subject is that of the superior—can compel him even unwilling to accept the prelacy, or forbid him to accept it, if there be a reason for doing so.

When consent is required, and the elect be present, the notification takes place immediately; if he be absent, it must be made within eight days, barring legitimate hindrance. If, at the expiration of eight days, the notification has not been forwarded, the electors are presumed to have omitted it through fraud or culpable neglect—unless they prove the contrary, and are punished by exclusion from the prosecution of the process, and are suspended for three continuous years from all benefices possessed in the church in which the election took place.[1] The notification may be intrusted to a procurator specially deputed for the office.

If, before the papers of election have reached the confirming prelate, the person elected in the presence of the electors withdraws his consent already given, the chapter may thereupon elect another, without awaiting the permission of the confirming prel-

[1] Miranda, II, q. 23, a. 10.

ate. The elect may afterwards recall his renunciation, with the consent of the vocals.[1] But if in the same hypothesis the superior has already received the papers, the chapter cannot proceed to a new election without his permission. Religious also may renounce their right, unless forbidden by superiors.[2] For although a religious has neither velle nor nolle contrary to the will of his superior, still the will of the latter is presumed to be that of the written law, unless the opposite is evident, as in the Order of Friars Preachers.[3]

The person elected must make known his acceptance or refusal within one month from the day he received the notification or permission of his superior when such is obligatory, and if he fails to do so he loses the right acquired by election, and the office becomes vacant.[4] If he refuses to accept the office, the chapter will proceed to another election within a month. The refusal of the person elected in no way prohibits his being reelected. In the Order of Friars Preachers, priors-elect must make known their acceptance or refusal within three hours from the receipt of the letters of confirmation.

II. If the person elected accept the proffered office, he acquires a real though still incomplete right to the said office, the jus ad rem to be changed to a jus in re by the confirmation of the election, and if qualified for the office in question, it is his privilege to exact confirmation from the superior, just as it is the latter's duty to give it. Confirmation, then, is the principal act of election, and immediately on its having been received there arises between the confirmed and the benefice a bond of spiritual matrimony. It also brings with it the power of jurisdiction, so that if a person should renounce an office after confirmation, the office does not become vacant by reason of the predecessor's death, but by reason of the renunciation of the person confirmed. Although confirmation confers jurisdiction, still the person confirmed does not acquire a right to exercise this jurisdiction until he has presented his letters of confirmation to the chapter.

Should the person elected interfere in the administration of his benefice before presenting the letters of confirmation to the chapter, all his administrative acts are invalid, and he is deprived of the benefice. This severe legislation, which concerns epis-

---

[1] cap. Si electio in VI.

[2] Oldr. ad. conf. 128, n. 7.

[3] Const. D. II, C. II.

[4] Rota, decis. 7, l. 2, conf. 5, cas. 477.

copal sees only, merits a brief notice. Innocent III[1] decreed that a bishop-elect but not confirmed cannot interfere in diocesan affairs, under penalty of losing ipso facto the right acquired by election. Exception was made for bishops outside of Italy, provided they were unanimously elected, and the utility or necessity of the diocese required their interference. In the Second Council of Lyons in 1274, Gregory X[2] forbade all elected persons to exercise the administration of their benefices by assuming the title of administrator, procurator, or the like—the punishment being deprivation of dignity. The French church contended that this legislation applied only to episcopal election and not to episcopal presentation, but since the reason for the prohibition is applicable to both cases, namely, to prevent an unworthy person from meddling in diocesan affairs, it includes both, for "ubi eadem est ratio, eadem est lex." Somewhat later Boniface VIII[3] promulgated a law still in force in regard to taking possession of episcopal sees and major benefices, in accordance with which bishops elected and confirmed must not enter into the administration of their sees before presenting letters of confirmation to the chapter of the cathedral church. In the United States, the letters must be delivered to the administrator of the diocese. On August 27, 1873, Pius IX published a Constitution in which he declared: 1° chapters can neither appoint temporarily vicars capitular nor remove them from office until the newly elected bishop shall have presented the apostolic letters of his promotion; 2° the constitution "Avaritiae" extends to candidates named and presented by heads of states in virtue of concordats; 3° the office of vicar capitular becoming vacant, the chapter should elect a successor, not however the bishop-elect, or persons nominated by civil power; 4° those offending against this law are punished by excommunication specially reserved to the Holy See, and privation of the revenues of their benefices; 5° the same penalties are incurred by the person elected or nominated, as well as by all those who give aid, counsel, or countenance. Moreover, the person elected or nominated loses all acquired right to the benefice, the acts exercised are invalid, and if he be a bishop he is further punished by suspension from pontifical ceremonies—this penalty also reserved to the Holy See. If the administrator

---

[1] Const. "Nihil."

[2] Const. "Avaritiae."

[3] Decret. "Injunctae."

[4] "Romanus Pontifex."

is elected bishop, he may continue the administration of affairs in virtue of his office already possessed at the time of election.

Some elections do not require confirmation, hence persons thus elected may enter upon the administration of office immediately on being elected. The Roman Pontiff, for instance, assumes full administration of the Church as soon as he is elected. Nearly all the generals of religious orders by reason of election are at the same time confirmed. Although elections of priors and provincials need confirmation, nevertheless in many provinces of the Order of Friars Preachers as soon as they have been elected, the provincials administer either as vicars—as in Spain, or as provincials—as in the provinces of the Indies.[1] But such jurisdiction is imperfect and quasi-conditional, and opposition can be made to the election itself, and action for cassation taken. Finally where there is a legitimately prescribed custom that a candidate-elect may administer before he has been confirmed, this custom obtains, and said person lawfully and validly exercises administration.[2]

According to common law persons elected not only may, but are bound to seek confirmation. Those whose confirmation rests with the pope, must set out for Rome within a month to obtain the required confirmation;[3] all others must request it within three months.[4] Those presented to a benefice by an ecclesiastic must receive confirmation within six months, if presented by a layman, within four months.[5] Allowances are made in all cases for legitimate hindrances. Confirmation may be sought by proxy, but not necessarily if the elect labor under an impediment, except when there is a question of papal confirmation.[6] If a friend, even though not commissioned, obtain the confirmation, it is valid if the person elected ratify the petition within three months.[7] Electors also may petition for the confirmation. In case of papal confirmation, two electors should accompany the one elected. Although it is the electors who request the confirmation in the Order of Friars Preachers, still the elect himself

---

[1] Peyr., c. 18, n. 2.

[2] Passerini, Ib., c. 33, n. 36.

[3] Cap. Cupientes in VI.

[4] cap. Quam sit ibidem.

[5] cap. Unico in VI.

[6] Passerini, Ib. n. 45.

[7] Barbosa, cap. Quam sit, n. 11.

may do so, and he is not to be censured for thus acting, since he is presumed not to be seeking his own so much as the public good.[1]

Persons-elect neglecting to attend to the matter of confirmation within three months forfeit their right, which returns to the chapter. Superiors may restrict this time limit for legitimate reasons.

A valid election must necessarily be confirmed by the superior, and if he refuse, he should be compelled to do so by higher authority, and a limit should be placed within which he must confirm, otherwise the higher authority should give the letters of confirmation.[2] No time is prescribed by common law, for the reason that it should be confirmed as soon as it is known to be valid; where special law sets a limit, it should be brief, and not exceed six months.

The constitutions of the Order of Friars Preachers say that provincials and generals may confirm or veto elections according as it seems best to them. This does not mean that they can per se veto a valid election, for the above concession does not bespeak absolute freedom, but the judgment of a prudent man, which should be regulated by law. Neither do the constitutions wish to derogate from common law, for they could not do so without special apostolic authority. Common law states that elections in no way canonically defective should be confirmed. Nevertheless, a superior may per accidens cass a valid election, for per accidens it is not necessary to confirm it. First, because of circumstances, for it could happen that the person elected—howsoever worthy—might be unacceptable to the authorities of the place in which the convent is situated, and because of this or other reasons grave scandal would arise. Secondly, if the common good of the order should require his services in another office incompatible with the prelacy in question.

Elections should be confirmed by the immediate superior of the person elected. Episcopal elections are confirmed by the pope. The pope or his legate a latere confirms the elections of all those immediately subject to the Holy See. The elections of generals that require confirmation are likewise confirmed by the pope or his legate a latere. The confirmation of other religious prelates pertain to their immediate superiors. In case of appeal the judge who pronounces the sentence either confirms or vetoes the election.

---

[1] Passerini, Ib. n. 47.

[2] Castellini, c. 14, n. 15.

Confirmation has no specified form, but may be given by oral or written word, or even an action bespeaking approval, such as installation or the like. Letters are necessary for confirmations coming from the Holy See, and also when other confirmations need to be proved. The confirming prelate must examine carefully both the election itself and the person of the one elected, for he must have a moral certitude that everything is conformable to law. Hastily given and uninvestigated confirmations may be objected to, and if justice demand it, they should be declared invalid,[1] and the superior loses the right of confirming the next prelate in that office, and is suspendid from his benefice. Regular superiors are not held to this investigation. In the Order of Friars Preachers a provincial must seek the counsel of discreets in confirming priors, and should he neglect to do so, he is to be punished, but the confirmation is valid.[2]

The superior must confirm the election of a worthy candidate.[3] This is true even if the electors had taken oath to elect the one best fitted, or even if there was a statute saying that the election of a worthy candidate should not prevail if one worthier were passed by, for such a statute—contrary to common law—is invalid, unless confirmed by the pope. The electors would sin mortally in not electing the one best fitted for the office.[4]

Confirmation given at the request of the parties concerned, or solemnly ex officio is a definitive sentence; but if given by summary judgment, it is an interlocutory sentence. Among regulars confirmation for the most part is given in a summary judgment, usually from report or testimonial letters. If made by interlocutory sentence, the superior may retract it and veto the election, but this cannot be done when confirmation is conferred by definitive sentence.[5] A superior residing outside of his territory cannot confirm an election solemnly ex officio, but only by summary judgment, for confirmation is a judicial act. Where the form in the last chapter on election in VI is observed, confirmation is always given by a definitive sentence, and hence cannot be pronounced outside of one's territory.

III. The acts of election and confirmation concluded, there next follows that of consecration. The former acts confer episcopal jurisdiction, while the latter brings with it the fullness of

[1] Ib., c. 14, n. 9.
[2] Passerini, Ib., n. 116.
[3] St. Th. 2a 2ae q. 63, art. 2, ad 3m.
[4] Passerini, Ib., n. 116.
[5] Ib., 169.

the priestly power—the completion of hierarchical orders. Former legislation conceded the right of both confirmation and consecration to the provincial metropolitan, who could delegate another bishop to perform the latter ceremony. In the present discipline no bishop can be lawfully consecrated except by the Roman Pontiff, or by his delegate specially commissioned for the purpose. The consecrator must therefore first of all assure himself of the delegation.[1]

If the consecration takes place outside of Rome, the bishop-elect by apostolic indult chooses as consecrator any bishop in communion with the Holy See. If it takes place in Rome permission is given him to choose either one of the cardinal bishops, or one of the four major patriarchs residing in Rome. Should no one of these accept, he may select any archbishop or bishop, but if his own metropolitan is in Rome at the time, the suffragan is obliged to request him to perform the ceremony. All consecrations that take place in Rome, must be conducted in a consecrated church or in the papal chapel.[2]

The ceremony is performed by three bishops, of whom one is the consecrator, and the other two assistants. A consecration, however, would be valid, and at times even licit, if conferred by one bishop, as is clear from indults of Gregory the Great, Gregory III, Innocent X, and Alexander VII. Bishops-elect of Latin America have an indult, in virtue of which they may be consecrated by two or three priests or canons, if the services of bishops cannot be obtained. If assistant bishops cannot be conveniently present, their places may be filled by two priests. In missionary countries, the consecrator may dispense with the assistance even of priests.[3] Previous to consecration a bishop-elect must take an oath of loyalty and obedience to the Holy See.

Bishops are bound to receive consecration within three months from the time of their confirmation, and should they neglect this duty without sufficient reason they must restore the profits meanwhile acquired; if they delay for another three months, they may be deprived of their episcopal sees.[4] Titular bishops lose their right of episcopal dignity if not consecrated within six months from their appointment.[5] Consecration, unless by special indult, must take place on a Sunday or the feast of an

[1] Ben. XIV. Conct. "In postremo."

[2] S. C. Rituum, n. V.

[3] Zitelli I. tit. 1.

[4] Conc. Trid. sess. 23, c. 2, de reform.

[5] Ben. XIV. Const. "Quum a nobis."

apostle or evangelist (dies natalitia)—not however on a feast commemorating events in the life of an apostle.[1] The Council of Trent prescribed that consecrations outside of Rome should take place in the cathedral church or at least within the province of the bishop-elect.[2]

Corresponding to episcopal consecration, perpetual abbots of monastic orders must within one year from the day of their election receive solemn benediction from the bishops in whose dioceses their monasteries are situated. If they are later transferred to another diocese, they are not held to seek this benediction a second time.[3] Prelates of nearly every other religious order, immediately on receiving and signing the letters of confirmation, become ipso facto superiors of the office for which they have been elected.

---

[1] S. C. Rituum, July 17, 1706.

[2] Ib.

[3] Ben. XIII. Const. "Commissi nobis."

APPENDIX

I

Manner of Electing a Sovereign Pontiff

On December 25, 1904, Pius X published a constitution "Vacante Sede Apostolica," in which he determined the present mode of papal election, and at the same time abolished all previous legislation on this point, except that contained in his former constitution "Commissum Nobis," and in that of Leo XIII "Praedecessores Nostri."

At the death of a pope the cardinal chamberlain takes charge of the papal household, in whose presence he juridically verifies the death of the pontiff by striking his forehead three times with a silver mallet, calling him by his baptismal name. The papal seals and the fisherman's ring are then broken. These acts, which are the legal evidence of a pope's death, are drawn up by a notary. The corpse is embalmed twenty-four hours after death, and on the following day borne to Saint Peter's, where it is exposed for three days in the chapel of the Blessed Sacrament. At the approach of evening the remains are interred in Saint Peter's, where they remain for one year bfore being taken to their final resting place.

Meanwhile all the absent cardinals are notified of the impending election by the secretary of the Sacred College, and those resident in Rome are obliged to wait ten days before they proceed with the election, assisting in the meantime at the solemn obsequies for the deceased pontiff. All the cardinals, unless detained by a legitimate impediment, are bound in virtue of holy obedience to obey the summons to the conclave. The funeral ceremonies completed, the cardinals on the tenth day assemble in Saint Peter's, where a Mass of the Holy Ghost is sung by the cardinal dean. This service over they immediately—or at evening, if they so prefer—go in procession to the conclave, a large walled off part of the Vatican palace. The aforesaid constitutions of Pius X and Leo XIII are then read, and after a brief sermon De Eligendo Summo Pontifice by the dean, the cardinals proceed to the cells assigned to them. Absent cardinals on reaching the city are admitted to the conclave at any time before the election is concluded. Each cardinal is accompanied by two attendants, either clerics or lay persons; in case of illness a third way be allowed. Other officials and attendants are admitted for the service of the cardinals in common, the conclave numbering in all about two hundred and fifty persons. The conclave closed, all communication with the outside is strictly forbidden, except in the presence of those prelates to whom the custody of the conclave has been assigned, and then only in an intelligible voice and idiom. All are equally sworn to secrecy concerning those things which relate to the election under pain of excommunication ipso facto incurred.

All cardinals, even those recently created but not yet vested with the insignia of office, enjoy active voice. Those excommunicated, suspended, and under interdict also have the right to vote. Cardinals not in deacon's orders are not admitted, unless by papal indult. Since the time of Urban VI in 1378 none but a cardinal has been elected, nevertheless any male christian who possesses the use of reason may be elected. The election of an infidel, heretic, schismatic, or female would be invalid.

The form of election is threefold, by compromise, by quasi-inspiration, and by secret scrutiny. The first two forms are the same as those explained above. The usual form is that of scrutiny or secret ballot, which is resorted to twice a day until an election takes place. For this mode of election three cardinals are chosen as scrutineers to preside over the voting, three others are chosen as revisors to attend to the count of their colleagues, and a final three as infirmarians to collect the ballots of the infirm, and of those lawfully detained from the hall of election.

Each cardinal writes his own and the name of his candidate on the ballot (Ego N. Cardinalis N. eligo in Summum Pontificem Reverendissimum Dominum meum Dominum Cardinalem N.), then seals and folds it so that the name of the candidate only is visible. Next it is folded so that no writing can be seen, and then, beginning with the dean, each cardinal takes his ballot between the thumb and index finger, bears it aloft to the altar before which stand the scrutineers, and on which is a large chalice covered with a paten. He kneels at the foot of the altar for a short prayer, then rising repeats in a clear and intelligible voice: "I call to witness Christ the Lord, who will judge me, that I elect the one whom before God I think ought to be elected." He next ascends the altar, places his ballot on the paten, from this drops it into the chalice, and returns to his place. If any cardinal present be unable to walk to the altar, the last scrutineer will go to him and receive his vote. The infirmarians then proceed to the cells of the infirm, if there be any, and bring their votes in a small sealed box with a narrow opening on the top to the scrutineers, who count and deposit them in the chalice.

The scrutiny concluded, the ballots are shaken up and counted one by one into another chalice, and should their number not correspond with that of the cardinals present, immediate recourse must be had to a new ballot. If the numbers agree, the chalice is brought to a table before the altar, the first scrutineer takes the ballots one by one from the chalice, unfolds each sufficiently to read the name of the candidate, then passes it to the second, who in turn passes it to the third, by whom the name is audibly announced to the cardinals. Each vocal has a list of the cardinals' names, and usually checks off the votes as they are read.

The ballots are counted, verified by the revisors, and burned in the presence of the cardinals. The so-called veto or "Exclusiva" against certain cardinals, occasionally exercised in the past by the powers of Austria, France and Spain was abolished by the present discipline, which also forbids any cardinal either directly or indirectly to introduce such a veto under penalty of excommunication reserved in a special way to the future pontiff. If no person receives the necessary two-thirds vote, the cardinals proceed immediately to another scrutiny, and continue this double scrutiny twice a day—in the morning and afternoon—until some one is canonically elected. When a candidate receives exactly two-thirds of all the votes—as did Benedict XV—the ballot of the pope-elect, distinguishable, like all the others, by a text of Scripture written on an outside fold, is opened to make sure that he did not vote for himself, for to ensure election a candidate must receive a two-thirds vote exclusive of his own.

If a candidate received the two-thirds vote, the cardinal dean approaches the newly elected pontiff and asks him whether he will accept the election and by what name he wishes to be known. If he accepts, all the cardinals arise, and the canopies of all the chairs are lowered, except that of the pope, who is conducted behind the altar where he is clothed in the papal garments. Returning to the pontifical chair, the cardinals pay him the first homage by kissing his foot and then his hand; they in turn receive the kiss of peace. The cardinal dean places upon his finger the fisherman's ring. These ceremonies over, the senior cardinal deacon proceeds to the loggia of St. Peter's facing the great piazza, and then announces to the assembled multitude the glad tidings of the election. The populace then enters the great basilica, where from the elevated loggia the new pontiff gives his first Apostolic Blessing Urbi et Orbi—to the city and the world.

The person thus elected, even though not yet in sacred orders, acquires full jurisdiction over the universal Church immediately on consenting, and becomes the Vicar of Christ on earth. If not already a bishop, he is consecrated at once by the cardinal bishop of Ostia, but this consecration confers power of orders only, not of jurisdiction. If the pontiff be a bishop, there takes place only the solemn blessing. The coronation, a mere ceremonial act, is received from the hands of the senior cardinal deacon on the following Sunday or holyday, from which date the years of the pontificate are computed. The final act—omitted since 1870—is the formal taking possession of the Lateran Basilica, the cathedral church of the Roman Pontiff, to which formerly he proceeded in solemn procession.

II

Method of Selecting Bishops in the United States

On July 25, 1916, the Sacred Consistorial Congregation prescribed the following legislation for proposing candidates for the episcopacy in the United States. At the beginning of the Lent of 1917, and thereafter every two years at the same time, each bishop shall indicate to his metropolitan the names of one or two priests, whom he considers worthy and fit for the episcopal ministry. Priests of another diocese or province may be proposed, but it is required sub gravi that those proposed be known personally and intimately by the person who proposes them. Together with the name of the candidate, his age, birthplace, present residence, and principal office shall be indicated.

The archbishops and bishops, previous to their own selection, shall ask of the diocesan consultors and permanent rectors the name of some priest whom they deem worthy and fit beyond others for the episcopal office. This interrogation shall not be made in an assembly, but separately to each, and enjoining on each sub gravi the obligation of secrecy, and of destroying all correspondence on the matter. This advice must not be disclosed, except perhaps at the meeting of the bishops, of which we shall speak later.

The bishops may consult other prudent men, even of the regular clergy, concerning the proposal of candidates or the obtaining of information as to their qualifications. They may, but are not bound, to follow any advice received, for they shall have to render an account to God alone in this matter. And to no other person besides the archbishop shall they make known the name or names they themselves propose.

On receiving from his suffragans the names of their candidates, the archbishop shall add his own, arranging all in alphabetical order, but making no mention of those who proposed them. He then dispatches a list of the names to the different suffragans, so that they may make inquiries about the qualifications of those, whom they do not know personally and with certain knowledge. These inquiries are to be made with the utmost secrecy, and should there arise a danger of the purpose of the investigation becoming public, they are to be dropped.

After Easter, on a day and at a place to be appointed by the archbishop, all the provincial bishops shall assemble with their metropolitan to select the names of those, whom they wish to propose to the Holy See for the episcopal ministry. They are to congregate without formality, as to a friendly gathering, that they may not attract attention or excite curiosity, especially of newspapers and periodicals. Then, having invoked the divine assistance, every one, including the archbishop, shall take an oath with hand on the Holy Gospels to observe secrecy, so that the bond by which all are bound may be the more sacred. This solemnity over, the regulations for conducting an election shall be read.

One of the bishops present having been chosen as secretary, a moderate discussion takes place, so that the more worthy and suitable of those proposed may be selected. The very importance of the matter urgently demands that the discussion be held and all things done as if Christ Himself were present and directing the affair, to the exclusion of every human consideration, but with discretion and charity, and with consideration only for the glory of God, for the supreme good of the Church, and the salvation of souls. The piety and religious obligations of all the prelates require that the proceedings be thus conducted.

The candidates should be of mature but not too advanced age, manifestly prudent in their ministerial work, extraordinarily sound in doctrine, devoted to the Holy See, but above all distinguished for their exemplary lives. Their business ability, personal status, natural disposition and health must also be considered. In a word it must be seen whether they possess all the qualities required of a good pastor to rule God's people with profit and edification.

When the discussion has been closed by the archbishop, the scrutiny then takes place. Those whom the bishops unanimously think should be removed from the list of candidates are not to be voted on; the others—even those most highly approved, shall be subjected to scrutiny by secret ballot, beginning with the first candidate in alphabetical order. The archbishop and all the bishops shall be given for each candidate three balls or pebbles, one white, another black, and a third of some other color. The first shall signify approbation, the second disapprobation, the third abstention from voting. Each prelate beginning with the archbishop shall deposit in a suitably prepared urn the ball which, before God and under grave obligation of conscience, he considers he should cast for the priest who is being voted on; the other two balls shall be dropped secretly into another urn. The scrutiny over, the archbishop assisted by the secretary shall in the presence of all count the balls, whatsoever their color, and consign the result to writing. Those who have been approved with full or an equal number of votes may, on request of a bishop, be submitted to a fresh scrtiny to decide which of them is to be preferred. Each prelate shall write the name of his choice on a ballot, and place it in the urn, and these shall be examined in the same manner as were the balls.

Although the Holy Father, on the vacancy of a see, reserves to himself to ask counsel of the bishops or Apostolic Delegate, so that he may select the one best fitted to govern the diocese in question, still the assembled bishops are free, nay are advised, to indicate at least generically which candidates are best suited for particular dioceses.

The secretary shall carefully note down all that was said and done at the meeting, and before the bishops separate he shall read and submit to their approval what he has written concerning the names proposed, the qualifications of the candidates, and the votes they have obtained. A copy of the acts, signed by the archbishop, secretary, and other bishops present, shall be transmitted in the safest way possible to the Sacred Congregation by the Apostolic Delegate. The acts themselves shall be preserved by the archbishop in the most secret archiepiscopal archives, but must be destroyed after a year, or even before should there arise a danger of the violation of secrecy.

The decree closes with the statement that both on the occasion of proposing a candidate or on the vacancy of a see—especially one of greater importance—the bishops may always have recourse to the Sacred Congregation or to the Holy Father himself, if they wish to give more precise information.

If at the beginning of Lent 1917, or in any of the biennial periods a bishop should be unable to propose names of candidates or to assist at the assembly of bishops, the coadjutor with right of succession may propose the names and take part in the subsequent deliberations, not however the auxiliary. Should the diocese be vacant no names are to be proposed, since the right to propose is granted to the bishop only, and not to the administrator. If at the same periods the metropolitan should be unable to preside at the convention of the bishops, he shall notify the Apostolic Delegate, who will appoint the senior bishop to attend to the functions of the archbishop. In the vacancy of the metropolitan see, the senior bishop himself shall obtain the required authorization from the Apostolic Delegate.

J. M. J. D.

SOURCES AND BIBLIOGRAPHY

Sources

Authentic Collections.
Gratian's Decretal and Private Collections.
Fourth Lateran Council.
Council of Trent.
Pontifical Documents.

Bibliography

Andrea, In sex libros Decretalium novella commentaria.
Antoninus, Summa.
Azorius, Institutionum moralium partes tres.
Barbosa, Opera Omnia.
Bargilliat, Jus Canonicum.
Baronius, De effectibus electionis etc.
Benedict XIV, Opera Omnia.
Boerius, De Jure Electionis.
Bonacina, De legitima summi electione pontificis.
Boudinhon, Catholic Encyclopedia.
Cajetan, Summa.
Capelli, Disputationes duae de summo pontifice.
Caramuelis, Hierarchia ecclesiastica.
Castellini, De electione et confirmatione canonica.
Castro, De electione.
Cavagnis, Institutiones juris publici ecclesiastici.
Craisson, Législation canonique et civile.
Cunou, Disputatio de electione.
Devoti, Institutiones canonicae.
Donatus, Rerum regularium praxis resolutoria.
Ferraris, Prompta Bibliotheca.
Frances, De intrusione tractatus.
Fontana, Constitutiones Ordinis Praedicatorum.
Garcia, De beneficiis.
Hostiensis, Summa.
Laymann, Jus Canonicum.
Lezana, Summa quaestionum regularium.
Mandagotti, Tractatus de electione.

Ojetti, Synopsis rerum moralium.
Passerini, De electione canonica.
Raymond, Saint, Summa.
Reiffenstuel, Jus canonicum universum.
Rodriguez, Summa.
Samuellini, Disputationum controversiae de canonica electione.
Schmalzgrueber, Jus canonicum universum.
Sebastianelli, Praelectiones juris canonici.
Smith, Elements of Ecclesiastical Law.
Sigismund, De electione.
Silvester, Electio.
Suarez, Opera theologica.
Sylvius, Electio.
Tabienensis, De electione.
Thomas, Saint, Summa Theologica.
Thomassin, Vetus et nova ecclesiae disciplina.
Wernz, Jus Decretalium.

Universitas Catholica Americae

Washingtonii, D. C.

S. Facultas Theologica

1916-1917

No. 2

TITULI

Deus Lux Mea

TITULI

quos ad Doctoratus Gradum in

JURE CANONICO

APUD
UNIVERSITATEM CATHOLICAM AMERICAE

Consequendum Publice Propugnabit

DANIEL MICHAEL GALLIHER
Sacerdos Ordinis Fratrum Praedicatorum
Juris Canonici Licentiatus

HORA IX A. M. DIE VI JUNII A. D. MCMXVII

I. De Vi Juridica Corporis Juris.
II. De Domicilio et Quasi-Domicilio.
III. De Ruthenis in Statibus Foederatis Americae Septentrionalis.
IV. De Incardinatione et Excardinatione.
V. De Potestate Ordinis et Jurisdictionis.
VI. De Privilegio Fori.
VII. De Coelibatu Clericorum.
VIII. De Litteris Testimonialibus et Dimissorialibus.
IX. De Romani Pontificis Electione.
X. De Cardinalium Origine, Creatione ac Numero.
XI. De Sacra Congregatione Sancti Officii.
XII. De Tribunali Sacrae Romanae Rotae.
XIII. De Modo Recurrendi ad Sacras Congregationes.
XIV. De Romani Pontificis Delegatis.
XV. De Metropolitis ac de eorum Potestate.
XVI. De Electione Episcoporum in Statibus Foederatis Americae Septentrionalis.
XVII. De Relationibus inter Episcopos et Regulares in Statibus Foederatis Americae Septentrionalis.
XVIII. De Jure Episcopi Ordanandi Religiosos.
XIX. De Vicario Generali.
XX. De Vicario Capitulari.
XXI. De Novitiatus Regimine.
XXII. De Distinctione Matrimonii inter Fideles.
XXIII. De Impedimento Mixtae Religionis et Disparitatis Cultus.
XXIV. De Impedimento Voti.
XXV. De Impedimento Affinitatis.
XXVI. De Impedimento Impotentiae.
XXVII. De Impedimento Criminis.
XXVIII. De Impedimento Vis et Metus.
XXIX. De Decreto "Ne Temere."
XXX. De Dispensationibus Matrimonialibus.
XXXI. De Convalidatione Matrimonii.
XXXII. De Sanatione in Radice.
XXXIII. De Privilegio Paulino.
XXXIV. De Transactionibus.
XXXV. De Arbitris.
XXXVI. De Foro Competenti.
XXXVII. De Judice.
XXXVIII. De Promotore Justitiae.
XXXIX. De Judice Delegato.

XL. De Actore et Reo.
XLI. De Advocatis.
XLII. De Actione Rescissoria.
XLIII. De Actione Reconventionali.
XLIV. De Cumulo et Extinctione Actionum.
XLV. De Introductione et Extinctione Instantiarum.
XLVI. De Libello.
XLVII. De Citatione.
XLVIII. De Litis Contestatione.
XLIX. De Probationibus.
L. De Testibus.
LI. De Instrumentis.
LII. De Praesumptionibus.
LIII. De Causis Incidentibus.
LIV. De Sententia.
LV. De Appellationibus.
LVI. De Re Judicata.
LVII. De Executione Sententiae.
LVIII. De Restitutione in Integrum.
LIX. De Processu Criminali.
LX. De Processu Matrimoniali.

Vidit Sacra Facultas:
Daniel I. Kennedy, O. P., S. T. M., p. t. Decanus.
Franciscus I. Coeln, Ph. D., p. t. a Secretis.
Vidit Rector Universitatis,
✠ Thomas I. Shahan, S. T. D.

VITA

Daniel Michael Galliher, the thirteenth son of Michael and Brigid Galliher, was born on August 11, 1883, at Hinsdale, in the Berkshire Hills of Massachusetts. His early studies were made in the public schools of his native town, and his higher classical education was received at Saint Laurent College, Montreal, Canada. He was graduated in 1909, and in September of that year entered the Order of Friars Preachers at Somerset, Ohio, where he made his religious profession on October 3, 1910. Thence he was sent to the Dominican House of Studies, at the Catholic University, Washington, D. C., to pursue the regular philosophical and theological course prescribed by his Order. Here he was ordained to the priesthood on June 23, 1915, by the Most Reverend John Bonzano, D. D., Delegate Apostolic. While at the University, Father Galliher followed courses in Canon Law under Doctor Bernardini, Mediaeval History and French under Doctors Robinson and Teillard, respectively.

www.ingramcontent.com/pod-product-compliance
Lightning Source LLC
LaVergne TN
LVHW050201080826
844660LV00012B/330

* 9 7 8 0 8 1 3 2 2 1 9 3 9 *